THE INTERNET TROUBLESHOOTER

HELP FOR THE LOGGED-ON AND LOST

Nancy R. John
Edward J. Valauskas

AMERICAN LIBRARY ASSOCIATION
CHICAGO AND LONDON 1994

Project editor, Arthur Plotnik

Cover design by Richmond Jones

Text design and composition by Dianne M. Rooney

The paper used in this publication meets the minimum requirements of American National Standard for Information Sciences—Permanence of Paper for Printed Library Materials, ANSI Z39. 48-1984. ∞

Library of Congress Cataloging-in-Publication Data

John, Nancy.
    The Internet troubleshooter : help for the logged-on or lost / by Nancy R. John & Edward J. Valauskas.
        p.   cm.
    Includes bibliographical references (p.) and index.
    ISBN 0-8389-0633-8 (alk. paper)
    1. Internet (Computer network)—Handbooks, manuals, etc.
I. Valauskas, Edward.   II. Title.
TK5105.875.I57J65   1994
005.7'1—dc20   94-11571

Printed in the United States of America

98 97 96 95 94   5 4 3 2 1

Contents

Introduction

The Internet Troubleshooter is for someone who is trying to use the electronic superhighway—also known to some as simply the Digital Hugeness—and is discovering, like all pioneers, that trouble lurks at every turn. This book is not an introduction to the Internet. Lots of recent books provide a general orientation, and new titles come out every week. Some of the best are listed in the short bibliography in the back of this book.

Since you are reading this book, you are probably among those in the intrepid jump-right-in school. And true enough, the only way to decide whether the Internet is for you is to try it. Based on the experience of millions of users, be prepared to like it when it works and to hate it when it seems not to. This book assumes that you have found at least a temporary way to the Internet and that you've already tried out a few Internet maneuvers. You've discovered that the road isn't as smooth as you thought.

Once you get onto the "information highway"—the metaphor that makes computer networking easier to understand—how do you get a flat tire fixed? Where's the motor club? Are there speed traps? This book helps Internet users solve some of the basic problems that occur as they cruise along. It addresses those potholes—glitches—that make "virtual life" both challenging and frustrating. It's meant to be your late-night companion when a puzzler makes you want to throw your keyboard out the window, or it's too late (or embarrassing) to call on your electronic neighbor. We all have earned some lumps in learning to live on the 'net—here's hoping you survive yours!

Still, to give you some context for understanding the wide variety of troubles, we will make a few general observations. Much has been written about why people get connected, and how. Not so long ago, answers were simple: you got connected because you were curious or because you had to.

And how you got connected was by working for a university or a research lab. In a short time, however, matters have become more complex. Now there are as many reasons to connect as there are ways to get connected.

Why Connect?

So, Question One: If you don't have your own connection, why should you take the trouble to get connected? The best reason is that the electronic superhighway is changing the way people communicate with each other, and, for the most part, for the better. Differences in time and space, personality, and interests can be conquered easily in the electronic world. Introverts and those who like to reflect on issues discover that the Internet allows time to consider and craft careful answers. Extroverts and those who like immediate feedback find that the Internet allows lightning-fast communication. Day people find they can talk to night people over the Internet. International collaboration becomes simpler. With millions of users and terabytes of data, the electronic highway has something for everyone.

There's a small universe of information out there. Some of it is actually good, even very current. Much is only available electronically. Some is available other ways, but more useful in digital form. "Eclectic" is the only term that covers the range. For example:

- Need a phone or fax number for your U.S. representative? The most current U.S. budget? Or a political speech? A Wide Area Information Server (WAIS—an Internet service) can help you.

- Which light broke through which window? If your Shakespeare is rusty, an Internet Gopher (another Internet tool) can help.

- What happens if you fall into a black hole? Technical papers on life (if you can call it that) inside one of Stephen Hawking's favorite subjects can be found at a computer at the Los Alamos National Lab. When does the electronic bus stop on this virtual highway to New Mexico? It never stops (unless the server crashes!).

- Somebody called you a trilobite! Should you be insulted? Where's a good roadside dictionary? A computer at Princeton can help.

Introduction

- What's the weather going to be like in Michigan this weekend? Weather machines at several computing sites can give you the latest forecast, even satellite images.

Of course, you can't find answers to everything on the Internet. Some files exist only for licensed users, some computers are inaccessible for many good reasons, and some folks will not write back if you send them a note. Life in virtual reality is a lot like life in reality, in spite of the hype. And for all the freeways on the Internet, you can run into tollbooths that affect the way you connect and your driving time.

Since getting connected and paying for one's connection are two common troubles, we'll give them some brief consideration in this introduction.

Getting Connected

Question Two: How do you get connected? This can be trickier than "why." The best way to get connected depends on your location and the equipment you will use as much as what you want to do with it. It also depends on how much you want to spend. For most individuals, a dedicated or wired connection is out of the question. Such a connection often costs several thousand dollars in addition to equipment costs. That leaves a telephone line, modem, and personal computer as the system of choice.

For those who want a learner's permit or training wheels, *The PC Internet Tour Guide*, *The Mac Internet Tour Guide*, and *The Windows Internet Tour Guide*, all from Ventana Press, include diskettes with Internet tools as well as a 30-day free trial dial-up connection to the Internet and instructions on its use. At around $25, these books are a bargain and are available at retail bookstores, sometimes at a discount. *Internet-in-a-Box* is another combination of Internet book and software. Due from O'Reilly & Associates in mid-1994, it will include software to connect, a subscription to the magazine *The Global Network Navigator*, and a special edition of Ed Krol's *The Whole Internet User's Guide & Catalog*. With this product, a computer, a 9600-baud modem, and a phone line, you can connect to the Internet.

For those who are sold on the concept and just want to get going, there are gateways to the Internet waiting to sign you up, among them CompuServe, Delphi, America Online (and its local spin-offs such as Chicago Online), The WELL, Apple's newly announced eWorld, the International Internet

Association, PSInet, and MCImail. There are regional carriers such as CICNet in the Midwest with its Dial Midwest program, and statewide programs such as netILLINOIS and the New York State Education and Research Network (NYSER-Net). Many access brokers act as intermediaries to your connection. To give only one example near the authors, the Chicago Library System has a contract with the Cooperative Library Agency for Systems and Services (CLASS) to provide electronic mail and other resources to Chicago area libraries, librarians, and library users. Other public libraries offer their users access by modem. These programs are advertised through community groups and users groups. Finally, in a growing number of cities, access to the highway is available through freenets, e.g., the Cleveland FreeNet, the Heartland FreeNet (Peoria), and Prairienet (Urbana). In short, there's no lack of ways to connect.

Some of these networks offer direct access to the Internet. Others try to keep you using their services and only offer an e-mail gateway to the Internet. In addition to e-mail, basic Internet services ought to include telnet, FTP, and Gopher. It's important to understand what kind of access you are getting for your money.

Costs

Question Three: How much does it cost? On commercial services, usually about $100–$150 to start up an account and $20–$50/month to use it regularly; the costs vary widely and, in general, are dropping. Most providers require a credit card to charge you monthly for your use. It is important to understand how you will be charged. Some providers use pricing schedules to encourage loyalty to their own services and to discourage the use of gateways to others. If you use one of these carriers and you subscribe to a BITNET LISTSERV list, you may have to pay a surcharge for each message you receive via the BITNET gateway. If a list is very busy, such as PACS-L, better raise the credit limit on your plastic because this can get quite expensive.

Here are some questions you should ask your network supplier: What services are available (e.g., electronic mail, file transfer protocol, Gopher, telnet)? How much do these services cost (e.g., fixed fee, per use, by the hour)? For example, some systems charge a fee for each message sent to or received from the Internet; or file transfer (FTP) may be free, but you may have to pay a charge based on the size of the

Introduction

file if you store it in your account. Is there a minimum charge you must pay each month whether you use the service or not? Is there a minimum amount of money you must spend before you can leave the system? How many points of presence (e.g., telephone numbers) does the vendor have? How easy and reliable will it be to connect? Will access to the Internet be direct, or through a gateway (gateways may limit access or functionality)? Does the gateway "batch-deliver" mail, or deliver mail as received? How much support will you get? Is training available? Is there a help line?

One Caveat

Since there are so many different entrance ramps to the superhighway, so many software configurations, it's just not possible for us to know exactly what your screen will look like. However, we know that many troubles are universal, and we've tried to address many of them here. We may not answer each question explicitly, but we'll try to head you in the right direction. Our examples represent different machines connecting to the Internet in different ways. When figures are used, we identify the type of connection and software in the captions.

Finally, we encourage you to submit your favorite "troubles" (and we would welcome solutions, too) for the next version of *The Internet Troubleshooter*.

Conventions used in the text

Boldface is used to highlight the troubles.

`Courier script` is used to identify characters that are to be typed as input.

Italic script is used for command names and titles of books.

<u>Underscored text</u> is used to identify subjects addressed in *The Internet Troubleshooter.* Check the index.

A single _ (underscored space) is used to indicate that internal spaces are not allowed in the user's formulation of the input, e.g., `Your_FirstName is Peggy_Sue.`

<...> denotes text that the user must supply, as it varies from user to user; e.g., user's address, name of <u>LISTSERV</u>.

Troubles have been numbered within each chapter, and references to particular troubles are made using first the chapter number, then the trouble number; e.g., "See **8.05**" means to see the fifth trouble in chapter 8.

Acknowledgments

We must acknowledge, first and foremost, all those intrepid Internet explorers who have given us the substance of this book. They remind us daily of what it was like when we first ventured out on the 'net, many invalid commands and bounced messages ago. We are grateful to our patient friends and colleagues who endured our whining and moaning, read and edited our prose, agreed to let us use them and their works as examples, and refused to believe that we couldn't get this book done in a hurry. We also managed to write this book in spite of our spouses, who offered us plenty of troubles along the way!

Troubles with the Internet (In General)

I know I'm supposed to change my password often, but I'm afraid I'll forget it.

Forgetting one's password is embarrassing; worse, it can keep you from being able to use your account. Smart networkers change their passwords often (see figure 1.1) and don't write them down on a post-it note stuck to their screens, or their desk calendars, or in their address books under P. Smart networkers use passwords just bizarre enough to keep someone from getting into their accounts by guessing; they also know some tricks so that they can remember their passwords. Some people can just remember random groups of letters and numbers. Others of us are not so adept, so here are some alternatives:

If you can recall some of the poems, sonnets, songs, or couplets you had to memorize in school, you have a great source of good passwords: 2RDIAW (Two roads diverged in a wood...), TITFPTMP (This is the forest primeval. The murmuring pines...), AVCTQPAO (*Arma virumque cano Troiae qui primus ab oris*), IWTYAT (It was twenty years ago today). You can easily rotate through a set of these. Those who want real words (and are willing to risk an electronic break-in) will use groups of words in a category—e.g., the names of the Beatles, sports, or automobiles—and rotate them. That way you know your password is one of three or four words.

```
New_East_Coast_Access (maf) Fri Mar 11 15:24:07 1994

    See News 1503 for cheaper NYC and Boston access information.

password_prudence (mo) Fri Feb  4 13:49:49 1994
    We've been notified by CERT (Computer Emergency Response Team)
    that they've observed a dramatic increase in reports throughout
    the internet of intruders monitoring network traffic.  This means
    that users who telnet into or out of the WELL might have had
    their passwords observed which means that they're vulnerable to
    their accounts being compromised.

    We should stress that this is not new; it's an ongoing, chronic
    problem that anyone who telnets to or from the WELL needs to be
    aware of.  No password (or other information) that is sent out
    over the network in clear text (unencrypted) can be considered
    absolutely safe, and large systems used by the general public
    are particularly attractive cracker targets.

    It's always a good idea to change your passwords often, and we
    strongly recommend this for those of you who do use telnet.
```

FIGURE 1.1
Opening welcome message from The WELL advising users about the importance of changing passwords frequently. This warning is directed specifically to those who are telnetting into The WELL.

1.02

I don't know what those nonalphabetic characters in my mail are.

It sounds like someone sent you an encrypted message. Many mail packages will compact or encode messages to assure their uncorrupted receipt. This is particularly true of longer messages and messages that contain files. Another possibility is that the sender shipped a version of the file that isn't eye-readable. For example, you may have been sent a PostScript file that is only intelligible to a PostScript printer or to special software that can decipher PostScript into text. If the message seems to have a mixture of eye-readable stuff interspersed with nonletter characters, you may have been sent a file that contains formatting characters from a word processing package. Here is an example of one of these files (see figure 1.2):

Troubles with the Internet (In General)

```
begin 600 RESPONSE.DOC
M,3DY-"TP,2TQ-PT*-PT*#0H-"E)E<W!O;G-E-("'1O($$5S(&5S(&)A<F)A<F$@
M5&EL;&&5T="="`H9&%%T960@@2F%N=6%R>2`Q,"P"P@,3DY-"TD@;VX@4F5S<@
M<F%F=$="'`Q.3DT+3`Q+3`V+"!087)T*"!087)7)T<'E`;F9O<B%087+AF5@@%
M M(#,$5.($$5E.65S(#0H-"C,C$B$$969I;FET96]N<PT*(#0H-"C]D=2T+"Q'1T*
M#0I(1S($YD<F%(%86=86%D($%5E($$5O=%%5$6D-"$86=$6$86=$@%3$$86=@
M_V%%(Q''(T<T+"`Q.3DT+$5V=H=V%],V5A=B`Q.3DY,CDY-RE-"!R;V$Y!V]R'
M=;R!A<PQ,CT"E4.($!R;V$Y!(S$$Q=R$5@;QG=(Z;V=(Q@Q@Y%X8Q@K8F)@@
M#0H-"C$9V$9&B;V1Y+W,F$Q9V`Q+CL@9&5&;F5D=6YK;@;FL@;P'15'$C2E
M(8$0E<$PP2@XD<9X.W-95P$$6D$#$$"P15'$Y65$86=92E86=<86=VY%9;E%
M=B=%0E<;E!/8D%$.C<M5#Q&15%);W0U22E5BE8..<"0P/$965@#;3T+5"P%5S
M<B='$D,;E!/8%D06$86=2$Q9&5%86=2%Y86=!86=2$5862$86=9V$86=$@%
```

FIGURE 1.2
An example of a Microsoft Word file (600 lines long, called *RESPONSE.DOC*) which has been encoded with uuencode into an e-mail message.

Once you've identified that you have one of these files, you can then try to convert it by printing it or using some conversion software, as appropriate. Or, you can ask your correspondent to send it again as an unencoded or ASCII text file (see **8.02, 8.04, 8.07**).

To ensure that you don't send these kinds of files:

1. You should always save a word-processed document as text, DOS-text, text only (no line endings), or text with line endings (used when tables or lists are in the text and you don't want them wrapped in a paragraph). Note: It's important to watch your margins so that you don't chop off the ends of your lines or words. An eighty-character or shorter line (e.g., 6.5 inches of 12 pitch) is a safe rule of thumb for most systems.

2. If you use a microcomputer mail package, change the settings so that files and long messages are not compacted or are compacted with a program your recipient has available. If there isn't a way to shut off the conversion and the software only converts files attached to mail, sometimes you can work around it by copying the document and pasting it into the text of the message.

1.03

Characters in my mail look like random series of punctuation marks. But I see them in lots of mail and files, so I'm beginning to think they have a meaning. What are they?

It's impossible to maintain any form of human communication that is emotionless and humorless. These combinations of punctuation marks and keyboard characters are known as "smileys," or "emoticons." They have been the subject of serious and not-so-serious research. They're used as a signal to display a mood, a feeling, an opinion. To observe these typographic signals, turn your head ever so slightly to the left and laugh! The fundamental smiley is a smile :-) followed by an unhappy smiley (an oxymoron?) :-(There are literally thousands of emoticons. Perhaps you'll invent some new ones to express yourself online. Collections of these symbols can be found in various electronic locales or in print in Peachpit Press's *The Smiley Dictionary*.

1.04

Sometimes, I see acronyms in electronic correspondence that I've never read elsewhere. What do BTW and OTOH mean?

As a form of shorthand, electronic epistolarians create acronyms for oft-repeated phrases, such as BTW, which translates to "by the way." Or OTOH, which equals "on the other hand." Always be wary of IMHO, or "in my humble opinion," because the author is sure to be verbose and proud, meaning IMNSHO. If you don't understand an abbreviation, ask. But make sure you aren't considered a PITA, or "pain in the.... "

Some other common acronyms include AFAIK (as far as I know), faq (frequently asked question/s), FWIW (for what it's worth), LOL (laughing out loud), and ROTFL (rolling on the floor laughing). If you ask too many dumb questions, some network type might tell you to RTFM (read the @*! manual), ;^) (wink).

1.05

I got connected to . . . and now I can't get out.

So many things to connect to and so many ways to get out. Let us list some common ways to exit:

```
bye            disconnect         esc-comma
cntl-C         done               esc-period
cntl-D         end                exit
```

Troubles with the Internet (In General)

```
log          PA-1         quit
logof        PA-2         X
logoff       pf3          .
logout       pf15         /*
off          q            :q
out          Q            :quit!
```

I'm worried about computer viruses, Trojan horses, bugs, and hackers. Should I be?

1.06

Of course. Safe computing is always an issue. However, if you are using the Internet just to send electronic mail and to transfer text files to or from your colleagues, the risks are minimal.

Your primary troubles with viruses and other malevolent programs will appear when you're downloading program files, especially shell scripts, and running them locally. Always check downloaded programs with a computer virus checking program. Keep your virus detection programs up-to-date and USE them. Forcing your virus software to check every program can slow down the initial execution of a program, but it is the only safe way to proceed.

Also, be careful of executing programs when you don't really know what they are supposed to do. An innocent-looking electronic holiday greeting card has been known to send messages to everyone in your electronic address book while you are watching it. This not only gives your friends a puzzling communication from you, but also wastes network resources.

Public and networked computing is never 100 percent safe. Nothing can take the place of frequent, complete backups of all local files. If you think about how long the backup process takes compared to how long it would take to reformat your hard disk and rekey in everything, it really is a small investment.

To keep hackers at a safe distance, don't share your password with anyone. Change your password often. Always change it if you suspect that someone may have learned it. Choose a password that's easy to remember and hard to guess (see **1.01**). If you are unexpectedly asked for your password on the network, think before you blithely type it in. You may be talking to a "Trojan-horse" program which is out on the net collecting the passwords of its victims. Anonymous FTP servers ask for userids to keep statistics, but they never ask for your personal password.

Troubles with E-mail 2

Electronic mail (see figure 2.1) is the most popular part of the electronic highway. It's fun, it's easy, it's entertaining, it'll change your life. So what could go wrong?

Too little mail.

2.01

This is *not* a problem for very long for most users. But if you want to start getting some mail to practice with, just subscribe to a couple of lists (see chapter 3).

Message   Edit   Send   Options   Window   Help

                    Mail from: Nancy R. John   Lines 1 to 16 of 16

Return-Path: <@UICVM.CC.UIC.EDU:nancy.john@UICVM.CC.UIC.EDU>
X-Sender: U31452@uicvm.uic.edu
Mime-Version: 1.0
Content-Type: text/plain; charset="us-ascii"
Date: Mon, 24 Jan 1994 15:22:08 -0600
To: U25112@ala.org
From: nancy.john@uic.edu (Nancy R. John)
Subject: test

This is a test.

* * * End of File * * *

FIGURE 2-1

Mac Eudora mail message as viewed by VM/CMS Rice Mail system. Message includes the most direct path back to sender, sender's real and alias addresses, type of message and compliance with the Internet Engineering Task Force Multipurpose Internet Mail Encoding (MIME), plus date, to:, from:, subject:, and body of text areas.

Too much mail.

Yep, this is a common problem. Here are some things to do to cut down on the volume of mail.

1. If you get a lot of mail from discussion lists, you can:

    (a) Unsubscribe. (Read the list's mail on a <u>news</u> <u>server</u> like NETNEWS, via Usenet or via <u>Gopher</u>, rather than subscribing yourself.)

    For BITNET <u>LISTSERV</u> lists:
    From CMS (Conversational Monitor System, a mainframe system that runs under the VM—Virtual Machine—Operating System to provide basic user services such as file management, file editing, and electronic mail) systems, use the interactive *tell* command and type:

    ```
    tell listserv at <hostname> signoff <listname>
    ```

    In other systems, send an electronic message addressed to

    ```
    listserv@<hostname> with the text
    ```

    ```
    signoff <listname>
    ```

    For complete freedom, issue (interactively or via e-mail) the global signoff from all <u>LISTSERV</u> lists to which you have subscribed with

    ```
    signoff (netwide
    ```

    The netwide signoff is available for BITNET <u>LIST-SERV</u>s because BITNET <u>LISTSERV</u> software has a listing available to it of all <u>LISTSERV</u> sites and lists.

    For Internet <u>LISTSERV</u> lists:
    Send an electronic message addressed to

    ```
    <listname>-request@<hostname> with the text
    ```

    ```
    signoff <listname>
    ```

    No netwide signoff is available for Internet <u>LISTSERV</u>s because management of lists is handled locally at each host site. The Internet <u>LISTSERV</u> software does not know of other host sites or lists, so it doesn't know where else to *signoff* a user.

(b) Stop a BITNET <u>LISTSERV</u> list from sending mail for a while, but keep the subscription active by issuing the command (interactively or via e-mail, as described at 1(a) above)

```
set <listname> NOMAIL
```

(c) Get just one (BIG) mailing a day by changing to the *DIGEST* option (if available) by sending the command (interactively or via e-mail, as described at 1(a) above)

```
set <listname> DIGEST
```

(See **7.10** for advice on handling large files.)

2. If you get a lot of mail and you care about it, you can organize the mail for better efficiency. Mail software allows you to sort things by sender, subject, and date, and to even assign priority. Mail can be filed into notebooks, mailboxes, folders, etc., where it can even be printed and later read on the bus home, at the dentist, or in an airport. Some mail software will let you download the mail to your hard drive or a diskette, where you can read and answer it offline. Offline means preparing the mail message(s) on your computer before you connect to the network.

3. If you get a lot of mail and aren't into mail, you can just let the stuff sit (or throw it out unanswered) and eventually correspondents will stop sending you mail. Of course, this won't work for mail from lists. It accumulates until you sign off, run out of space, or close your account.

Bounced mail.

2.03

It happens to us all sooner or later. When mail is bounced back to you, you need to read the message.

1. Is the node down? Check to see if the network software will continue to try to deliver your mail; often it will (see **2.04**).

2. Is the user's account too full to receive the mail? You'll need to try again when you think your pen pal has cleaned up and made some room for new mail. Or, you can always contact your colleague and tactfully suggest some disk-clearing.

3. Or does the message suggest that you made a mistake in typing or copying the address, e.g., USER UNKNOWN, UNKNOWN DOMAIN, etc.? Double-check the address (see figure 2.2 and Trouble **2.05**).

```
Return-Path: <>
Received: from UICVM (NJE origin SMTP@UICVM) by UICVM.CC.UIC.EDU (LMail
         V1.2a/1.8a) with BSMTP id 0587; Sun, 13 Mar 1994 16:06:25-0600
Received: from SSCVX1.SSC.GOV by UICVM.UIC.EDU (IBM VM SMTP V2R1) with
TCP;
     Sun, 13 Mar 94 16:06:23 CST
Date:      Sun, 13 Mar 1994 16:06:32 -0600 (CST)
From:      Postmaster@SSCVX1.SSC.GOV
Subject:   Undeliverable Mail
To:        <U31452@UIC.EDU>

Bad address -- <valauskas>
Error --
      %MAIL-E-NOSUCHUSR, no such user VALAUSKAS

Start of returned message

   Received: from UIC.EDU by SSCVX1.SSC.GOV with SMTP;
           Sun, 13 Mar 1994 16:06:30 -0600 (CST)
   Received: from UICVM.CC.UIC.EDU by UIC.EDU (IBM VM SMTP V2R1)
       with BSMTP id 5327; Sun, 13 Mar 94 16:06:11 CST
   Received: from UICVM (NJE origin U31452@UICVM) by UICVM.CC.UIC.EDU
(LMail
 V1.2a/1.8a) with BSMTP id 0583; Sun, 13 Mar 1994 16:06:11 -0600
   Date:      Sun, 13 Mar 94 16:05:53 CST
   From:      Nancy John <U31452%UICVM@UIC.EDU>
   Subject:   Greetings!
   To:        valauskas@sscvx1.ssc.gov

   Ed,
   How's that neutrino project going?
   Nance

End of returned message
```

FIGURE 2.2
Mail returned by the postmaster at the Internet domain `sscvx1.ssc.gov` because account of user is no longer valid.

I received a message back that my message could not be delivered. What do I do?

Read the message carefully. It may be a warning of a temporary problem. A part of the network may be down. In this case the message is a courtesy to let you know, in case the message is time-dependent, that your message is in a queue waiting for delivery (see figure 2.3). Other times, it will alert you to a more serious problem, and you'll need to try again later or, more likely, to contact your recipient another way.

```
Return-Path: <LISTSERV@UICVM.CC.UIC.EDU>
Received: from UICVM.UIC.EDU (NJE origin LISTSERV@UICVM) by
UICVM.CC.UIC.EDU (LMail V1.2a/1.8a) with BSMTP id 3308;
Fri, 25 Mar 1994 17:57:04 -0600
Date: Fri, 25 Mar 1994 17:57:03 -0600
From: BITNET list server at UICVM (1.7f) <LISTSERV@UICVM.UIC.EDU>
Subject:    ALA-WO: error report from DEPAUL
To:    ALAWASH@ALAWASH.ORG,
Nancy John <U31452@UICVM.BITNET>
X-LSV-ListID: None

The enclosed mail file, found in the ALA-WO reader and shown under the
spoolid 7220 in the console log, has been identified as a possible
delivery error notice for the following reason: mail subject indicates a
delivery problem.

---------------------- Message in error (248 lines) -----------------
Date: Fri, 25 Mar 1994 17:55 CST
From: <POSTMASTER@DEPAUL>
Subject: Returned  Network  Mail
To:    ALA-WO@UICVM
Original_To: BITNET%"ALA-WO@UICVM.BITNET"

Your mail is being returned to you.
Reason for return is:
%MAIL-E-OPENOUT, error opening !AS as output -RMS-E-CRE, ACP file create
failed
-SYSTEM-F-EXDISKQUOTA, disk quota exceeded
Returned mail follows:
------------------------------
Received: From UICVM(MAILER) by DEPAULO with Jnet id 1540
for abcdefg@DEPAUL; Wed, 23 Mar 1994 17:46 CST Return-Path: <owner-ala-
wo@UICVM.CC.UIC.EDU> Received: from UICVM.UIC.EDU (NJE origin
LISTSERV@UICVM) by UICVM.CC.UIC.EDU
```

FIGURE 2.3

This message from a mailer indicates that the mailer is trying to deliver the mail it has received. It has been unable to accomplish this because the recipient's disk space is full.

I have a business card with the e-mail address of someone, but the mail to her keeps bouncing back.

The simple answer may be that the address is wrong or has changed. Here are some other things to check:

1. Make certain you have not mixed up the numeral "1" and the letter "l."

       pacs-l@uhupvm1

   is P-A-C-S-hyphen-L-atsign-U-H-U-P-V-M-one

2. Make certain that you have not confused the number 0 and the letter O.

       g0094@applelink.apple.com

   is G-zero-zero-nine-four-atsign-A-P-P-L-E-L-I-N-K-period-A-P-P-L-E-period-C-O-M

3. Make certain the address is complete. U.S. Internet addresses always have at least THREE parts:

       userid@domain.domain_type

   Top level U.S. domain_types are .com, .edu, .gov, .mil, .net, .org. Many U.S. addresses take the format userid@node.domain.domain_type. Addresses for other countries, and some U.S. addresses, end in a code for the country. Sample codes are .us (United States), .uk (United Kingdom), .th (Thailand), .br (Brazil), .de (Germany), etc.

4. Make certain that you have typed the address *exactly* in terms of upper- and lowercase, spacing, and punctuation.

   CompuServe accounts are a known special case. The comma in a CompuServe address must be changed to a period in order to send from the Internet to CompuServe. So if you know of someone as 12345,678 in CompuServe, then the Internet form of the address should be

       12345.678@compuserve.com

How can I find an address?

Not so long ago, your only choice was to ask the person. Increasingly various directories, print and electronic, make finding addresses easier. One of the fallacies is that somehow electronic address books are more accurate and up-to-date than print directories. While that may be true to some extent, it doesn't mean that they are up-to-date. It is, however, likely that the electronic address is the most accurate information, assuming that the account is still open, since most of these directories were created to support electronic communication. The inaccuracy of network-accessible data was proved to the authors as we requested the permission of the real people in our examples to use their entries as illustrations for the answer to this question. They all cited inaccuracies in the data we found out on the 'net.

Notre Dame University maintains on its Internet Gopher a gateway to many online telephone directories. To get to this directory, point your Internet Gopher tool toward gopher.nd.edu and look under

```
Non-Notre Dame Information Sources/Phone
Books--Other Institutions/
```

Many organizations support remote access to local phone books via software that allows networkers to search for addresses. Here are four other useful approaches:

```
Name: Peter Scott Graham +PSG1+, Library Administration, Administration, Faculty and
Staff Directory, Rutgers University, New Jersey, US
"Peter Scott Graham +PSG1+"
commonName:           Peter Scott Graham +PSG1+
surname:              Graham
title:                Assoc Univ Libr-Tech and Autom Svc
description:          Also call 2-5908 (Lib. Tech. Svcs. Bldg
postalAddress:        Room 0271, Alexander Library,
                         College Av Campus,
                         Rutgers University,
                         New Brunswick, NJ 08903
telephoneNumber:     +1 908-932-7505, +1 908-932-7505
userid:              +PSG1+
mail:                psgraham@gandalf.rutgers.edu
lastUpdateTime:       930929234303Z
```

FIGURE 2.4

Results of a WHOIS search conducted via Internet Gopher at `sipb.mit.edu`.

1. WHOIS. The <u>Internet Gopher</u> at `sipb.mit.edu` maintains a list of WHOIS servers under `/pub/whois/whois-servers.list`. Your e-mail software may support use of WHOIS to find addresses, or may prefer use of one of the other server protocols. The WHOIS server at `rs.internic.net` is probably the most valuable of the Internetwide servers (see figure 2.4).

2. NETFIND. This tool/gateway allows you to search across the Internet in many separate directories with a single command. You must <u>telnet</u> to a server-host, such as the University of Colorado at Boulder's

   `bruno.cs.colorado.edu`

   and login as `netfind`, then follow the screens to learn how to search for an address (see figure 2.5).

Troubles with E-mail

```
SunOS UNIX (bruno)
Login as `netfind' to access netfind server
login: netfind

========================================================
Welcome to the University of Colorado Netfind server.
========================================================

Alternate Netfind servers:
        archie.au (AARNet, Melbourne, Australia)
        bruno.cs.colorado.edu (University of Colorado, Boulder)
        dino.conicit.ve (Nat. Council for Techn. & Scien. Research, Venezuela)
        ds.internic.net (InterNIC Directory and DB Services, S. Plainfield, NJ)
        eis.calstate.edu (California State University, Fullerton, CA)
        hto-e.usc.edu (University of Southern California, Los Angeles)
        krnic.net (Korea Network Information Center, Taejon, Korea)
        lincoln.technet.sg (Technet Unit, Singapore)
        malloco.ing.puc.cl (Catholic University of Chile, Santiago)
        monolith.cc.ic.ac.uk (Imperial College, London, England)
        mudhoney.micro.umn.edu (University of Minnesota, Minneapolis)
        netfind.anu.edu.au (Australian National University, Canberra)
        netfind.ee.mcgill.ca (McGill University, Montreal, Quebec, Canada)
        netfind.if.usp.br (University of Sao Paulo, Sao Paulo, Brazil)
        netfind.oc.com (OpenConnect Systems, Dallas, Texas)
        netfind.vslib.cz (Liberec University of Technology, Czech Republic)
        nic.uakom.sk (Academy of Sciences, Banska Bystrica, Slovakia)
        redmont.cis.uab.edu (University of Alabama at Birmingham)

Netfind now lets sites customize how to search for users there, and can
interoperate with X.500, WHOIS, and PH.  For more information, retrieve
the file pub/cs/distribs/netfind/Netfind.WP.URLs from
ftp.cs.colorado.edu.

A paper describing Netfind's data gathering framework and algorithms is
available by anonymous FTP from ftp.cs.colorado.edu, in
pub/cs/techreports/schwartz/PostScript/Netfind.Gathering.ps.Z or
pub/cs/techreports/schwartz/ASCII/Netfind.Gathering.txt.Z.

I think that your terminal can display 24 lines.  If this is wrong,
please enter the "Options" menu and set the correct number of lines.

Top level choices:
        1. Help
        2. Search
        3. Seed database lookup
        4. Options
        5. Quit (exit server)
-->
```

FIGURE 2.5

Opening screen from an NCSA/BYU Telnet 2.5 session at bruno.cs.colorado.edu.

3. PH servers. Some sites use the server package PHSERVE (see figure 2.6) to support searching by PH, in turn supported by some mail software packages, notably Eudora. PHSERVE is also available via gateways such as <u>Internet Gopher</u>. Searching is limited to a single server, which equates to a single organization, but can be very useful if that site is where your would-be correspondent is located.

```
From UIUCVMD(PHSERVE): * ----------------------------------------
From UIUCVMD(PHSERVE): * name: wedgeworth robert
From UIUCVMD(PHSERVE): * phone: (217) 333-0790
From UIUCVMD(PHSERVE): * address: 1408 w gregory rm 23, MC 522
From UIUCVMD(PHSERVE): * : 1408 w gregory dr
From UIUCVMD(PHSERVE): * : urbana, il 61801
From UIUCVMD(PHSERVE): * department: library admin
From UIUCVMD(PHSERVE): * title: univ librn, prof of lib & info sci
From UIUCVMD(PHSERVE): * email to: rwedge@uiuc.edu (rwedge@vmd.cso.uiuc.edu)
From UIUCVMD(PHSERVE): * ----------------------------------------
```

FIGURE 2.6
Results of a VM/CMS interactive *tell* command
(tell phserve@uiucvmd robert wedgeworth) search of PHSERVE@UIUCVMD.

4. *Finger. Finger* is useful at finding out an address if you know what Internet domain someone uses to get access to the Internet. It will also tell you who is currently signed on to the domain. *Finger* has caused some concern because it reveals the last time the user logged on (see figure 2.7). It has some curious uses, too. For example, *finger* is known to point at various computer-controlled and -accessed soft-drink vending machines.

```
       Name: John, Nancy R.
 Department: Library
      Title: Assistant University Librarian
      Phone: 996-2716
        Fax: 413-0424
    Address: 1-280 LIB
           : Campus MC 234
  E-mail to: Nancy.John@uic.edu
ADN Account: U31452@UICVM
Last login was on 03/13/94.
Connected from john.lib.uic.edu.
```

FIGURE 2.7
Results of a *finger* of uicvm.uic.edu using Eudora's *finger* command. Note that *finger* may reveal the last time the user was logged on, and the complete local address of a machine on the 'net.

Troubles with E-mail

My replies go astray.

Learning when to use (or not to use) the reply feature of your electronic mail software is important for responsible network behavior. More embarrassment occurs from the broadcast of private replies than from any other network novice error. Mail systems should allow you to read the header of a piece of mail to see who sent it and to whom it is going. Practice reading these headers (see figure 2.8). Train yourself to do this always with your e-mail to avoid virtual blushing.

```
001 Return-Path: <@UICVM.CC.UIC.EDU,@CUNYVM.CUNY.EDU:G0094@APPLELINK.APPLE.COM>
002 Received: from CUNYVM.CUNY.EDU (NJE origin MAILER@CUNYVMV2) by UICVM.CC.UIC.EDU
(LMail V1.1d/1.7f) with BSMTP id 8944;
003 Tue, 7 Sep 1993 12:06:11 -0500
004 Received: from CUNYVM (NJE origin SMTP@CUNYVM) by CUNYVM.CUNY.EDU (LMail V1.1d/1.7f)
with BSMTP id 0565;
005 Tue, 7 Sep 1993 13:06:59 -0400
006 Received: from guardian.apple.com by CUNYVM.CUNY.EDU (IBM VM SMTP V2R2) with TCP;
007 Tue, 07 Sep 93 13:06:56 EDT
008 Received: from [90.1.0.8] by guardian.apple.com with SMTP (5.65/22-Jun-1993-eef) id
AA22751;
009 Tue, 7 Sep 93 09:15:49 -0700 for
010 Received: by alink-gw.apple.com (921113.SGI.UNSUPPORTED_PROTOTYPE/28-May-1993-eef) id
AA10926;
011 Tue, 7 Sep 93 09:11:06 -0700 for U31452%UICVM.BITNET@cunyvm.cuny.edu

012 Date: 07 Sep 93 15:49 GMT
013 From: G0094@AppleLink.Apple.COM (Valauskas, Edward,GOV)
014 Subject: bibliography request
015 To: U31452%UICVM.BITNET@cunyvm.cuny.edu
016 Message-Id: <747418266.7711605@AppleLink.Apple.COM>
017
018 Nance:
019
020     FYI
021
022     ed
```

FIGURE 2.8

Anatomy of this message sent from Apple's AppleLink system to a node on BITNET:

lines 012-022: the body of the message as composed by the AppleLink software including the date (line 012), the sender's address (line 013), the subject (line 014), the recipient's address (line 015), the message id (line 016), and start of the actual message (lines 017-022);

lines 001-012: the header of the message best read upward as follows: line 012 shows that the original note was sent at 15:49 Greenwich Mean Time, or 8:49 a.m. in California; lines 010-011: message received by the Apple gateway to the Internet at 9:11 a.m. and sent on; lines 008-009: message received by Apple Internet server at 9:15 a.m. and sent on; lines 006-007: received from the Apple server by CUNY's Internet/BITNET gateway at 1:06 p.m. (10:06 California time) and sent on; lines 004-005: message received 3 seconds later from the BITNET server with the information that UICVM can be reached via the Internet domain at UICVM.CC.UIC.EDU; lines 002-003: message received from the CUNY Internet server by UICVM's Internet server at 12:06 p.m. (10:06 California time) and delivered with information about the return path (line 001) for a reply to follow.

Use of special reply features can result in sending replies appropriately. Commands such as `replyto`, `reply from`, and `reply all` or similar commands or parameters should allow your mail software to perform well. Otherwise, send a new message rather than misuse the reply command (see figure 2.9).

```
Anatomy  of  a  header:

 who  sent  and  how  many  lines:
                         Mail from: Nancy R. John       Lines 1 to 16 of 16
         Return-Path: <@UICVM.CC.UIC.EDU:nancy.john@UICVM.CC.UIC.EDU>
alternate  address  for  sender:
         X-Sender: U31452@uicvm.uic.edu
         Mime-Version: 1.0
         Content-Type: text/plain; charset="us-ascii"
         Date: Mon, 24 Jan 1994 15:22:08 -0600
address  mail  was  sent  to:
         To: U25112@ala.org
preferred  address  for  reply:
         From: nancy.john@uic.edu (Nancy R. John)

         Subject: test

         This is a test.


         * * * End of File * * *
```

FIGURE 2.9a
Mail message sent from Mac Eudora 2.0.1 viewed from CMS Rice Mail.

```
                       Mail from: Nancy John (312) 996-27  Lines 1 to 18 of 225
                                                              More:    +
Return-Path: <@UICVM.CC.UIC.EDU:U31452@UICVM.CC.UIC.EDU>
Date: Sat, 15 Jan 1994 13:06:17 CST
From: "Nancy John (312) 996-2716" <U31452@UICVM>
To:    <U25112@uicvm>
Subject: Fwd: keystroke monitoring, fyi

probably of interest
------------------------Original message---------------------------
Return-Path: <@UICVM.CC.UIC.EDU:owner-academy@UICVM.CC.UIC.EDU>
Received: from UICVM.UIC.EDU (NJE origin LISTSERV@UICVM) by UICVM.CC.UIC.EDU
         (LMail V1.1d/1.7f) with BSMTP id 5362; Sat, 15 Jan 1994 09:52:41 -0600

Date:        Sat, 15 Jan 1994 09:49:20 CST
Sender:      Academic Town Hall <ACADEMY@UICVM.BITNET>
From:        "James.A.Danowski@uic.edu" <U45571@UICVM.BITNET>
Subject:     keystroke monitoring, fyi
```

FIGURE 2.9b
Why replies go astray: How many To/Sender:'s and From:'s can you see, and which one(s) will your mail software use? (Mail forwarded using CMS mail viewed with CMS Rice Mail.)

Troubles with E-mail

```
Return-Path: <@UICVM.CC.UIC.EDU:nancy.john@UICVM.CC.UIC.EDU>
X-Sender: U31452@uicvm.uic.edu
Mime-Version: 1.0
Content-Type: text/plain; charset="us-ascii"
Date: Fri, 11 Feb 1994 15:40:26 -0600
To: U25112@uicvm (Edward Valauskas)
From: nancy.john@uic.edu (Nancy R. John)
Subject: Re: LA meeting

>Date: Fri, 11 Feb 94 13:52 CDT
>To: nancy.john@uic.edu
>From: our_friend@UTXVM.CC.UTEXAS.EDU
>Subject: Re: LA meeting
>
>(text starts here...)
```

```
F1 =Help      F2 =Delete   F3 =Quit     F4 =Print    F5 =Reply    F6 =Switch
F7 =Backward  F8 =Forward  F9 =Save     F10=MenuBar  F11=Next     F12=Cancel
====>
```

FIGURE 2.9c

Your mail software should only see one From: and one To: when it replies to this message because the sender's software has added the > character in front of the From: and To: in the forwarded message. (Mail forwarded with Mac Eudora 2.0.1 and viewed in CMS Rice Mail.)

My replies keep bouncing back to me.

2.08

This usually means that the sender's mailer doesn't put a complete address in the "From:" field. This happens mostly with mail sent from local area networks (LANs) where mail within the LAN doesn't require complete addresses. It usually indicates a need to install some added features in the LAN's mail server. Or it may mean that the sender needs to invoke a different set of commands to identify to the software that this is a message destined for delivery outside the LAN.

If the mail is from a correspondent in another country (see figure 2.10), it may not have a complete enough international address or, sometimes, the address protocol will differ, so that the address is in a different form than your mailer expects.

```
Return-Path: <@UICVM.CC.UIC.EDU:tasnporn@IPIED.TU.AC.TH>
Received: from UICVM (NJE origin SMTP@UICVM) by UICVM.CC.UIC.EDU (LMail V1.1d/1.7f)
with BSMTP id 6751; Fri, 7 Jan 1994 04:56:39 -0600
Received: from chulkn.chula.ac.th by UICVM.UIC.EDU (IBM VM SMTP V2R1) with TCP; Fri,
07 Jan 94 04:56:36 CST
Received: from ipied.tu.ac.th.tu.ac.th by chulkn.chula.ac.th with smtp (Smail3.1.28.1
#12) id m0pIEsE-0003GxC; Fri, 7 Jan 94 17:56 BKK
Date: Fri, 7 Jan 1994 17:06:20 +0700 (GMT+0700)
From:   Tasanaporn  Gadavanij  <tasnporn@ipied>
Subject: Happy New Year to you too!
To: Nancy John <u31452@uicvm.uic.edu>
Message-Id: <Pine.3.07.9401071720.B16571-b100000@ipied> Mime-Version: 1.0
Content-Type: TEXT/PLAIN; charset=US-ASCII
```

FIGURE 2.10a

Header of international mail with only local network address appearing in the `From:` field; complete address appears in the `Return—Path` statement in the header.

```
To:   Tasanaporn  Gadavanij  <tasnporn@ipied>
From: n.john@uic.edu (Nancy R. John)
Subject: Re: Happy New Year to you too!
Cc:
Bcc:
X-Attachments:
```

FIGURE 2.10b

This message would be returned because the incomplete `To:` address resulting from using the *reply* command in Eudora would keep it from being delivered.

The solution is to check the "To:" field in the reply and to edit it to include a complete address in the format your mailer understands. Or, you may decide it's just easier to send a new message rather than to use the reply feature.

There are two other explanations:

1. Some mail programs automatically include, or can be set to include, the sender in the recipient list. As a sender, you might choose this setup because your mail package can't keep a copy of outgoing mail.

2. If you have several addresses or aliases, you may find that you will get a copy of your reply. The mail software might not recognize the address used for you in the original mail message as your address (see figure 2.11). It sent you a reply because it thinks that you are someone else.

Troubles with E-mail

```
Date: 25 Mar 94 16:52 GMT
From: G0094@AppleLink.Apple.COM (Valauskas, Edward,GOV)
Subject: From Ron Watson
To: U31452@UICVM.UIC.EDU

Nance:

From Ron W.

Ed

--

Item 3600756        25-Mar-94    07:44

From: ECZ5RON@MVS.OAC.UCLA.EDU@INTERNET#

To:   G0094 Valauskas, Edward,GOV

INTERNET# Document Id: <9403251543.AA16993@alink-gw.apple.com>

-----------------------------------------------------------------------
Sub: Your IFLA journal article
```

FIGURE 2.11a
Addresses can take several forms because of the use of aliases. Mail servers know all the various versions of a person's address and deliver the mail anyway. This mail was sent to the recipient's alphanumeric address, but as you can see below this may present an interesting problem when the recipient uses the *REPLY ALL* command below.

```
To: G0094@AppleLink.Apple.COM (Valauskas, Edward,GOV),
U31452@UICVM.UIC.EDU  (Nancy  John)
From: n.john@uic.edu (Nancy R.  John)
Subject: Re: From Ron Watson
Cc:
Bcc:
X-Attachments:
At 16:52 3/25/94 +0000, Valauskas, Edward,GOV wrote:
NNance:

Thanks!

>From Ron W.

>Ed

>--
```

FIGURE 2.11b
Mac Eudora's *REPLY ALL* command doesn't recognize the numeric address of this user as the same as the name address. Hence the system has included the user in this reply unintentionally.

I'd like the original message in my reply.

This is a feature of the electronic mail software you use. Most systems allow you to specify a default (always include the original text) or override that default, e.g., `reply notext`. Check the software or system documentation for your local reply conventions.

How do I keep the original message from going into the reply?

This, too, is a feature of the electronic mail software you use. Usually you can specify a default (always exclude the original text) or override that default, e.g., `reply text`. Again, check the software or system documentation for your local reply conventions.

My friends say my messages don't look nice. Words break in funny places and sometimes the end of my lines wrap funny or don't show up at all.

Maybe your friends don't appreciate your creativity. But again, this is a feature of the mail software you use. Some software programs are full-screen and support word wrapping like a word processor. Other systems use line-based input requiring the typist to end the line explicitly. Some software packages support both types of input depending on the commands you use. You need to understand which type of system you are using, and what defaults are active for the system you are using. Most personal computer mail programs support word-processor type manipulation of text. Mainframe mail software can be less flexible, although often there is a way to make them more friendly; for example, the "power typing" mode available in CMS systems using the CMS mail or Rice Mail software. One way to experiment is to send some mail to yourself to see what it looks like.

I got only part of a note that was sent to me.

It's difficult to know at which end the problem exists. Maybe your correspondent didn't send you the whole message. Or maybe you did get the whole thing but can only see part of it. Did you scroll all the way to the bottom of the message?

Does the message header tell you how many lines it contains, and can you see that many? Some systems limit how much of the message can be seen before the message is received or filed by the recipient. Finally, you can always ask your correspondent to send it again.

A friend sent me a file with a note. I can't find the file.

2.13

Again it's difficult to know at which end the problem exists, but there are some logical places to start. Many mail programs treat files differently than mail, so the file may be stored elsewhere. For example, the mail software package may only be able to read certain file types, and may leave other files on the mail server. The result may be that only mail is downloaded to a personal computer while files remain up on the mail server machine. The files must be moved by entering commands, such as FTP. Also, personal computer mail software packages will often take an attached file and save it directly to your hard disk, so be sure to look around to see if the file is already filed there.

The contents of a note/file I got are all scrambled and funny looking. What's wrong?

2.14

Welcome to the wonderful world of compression and encryption (see **1.02** and **8.02, 8.04, 8.07**). Mail packages often compress or encrypt files or longer mail messages to assist with speedy transfer and to limit the possibility of the file or message being corrupted during its travels across the network. To uncompress or unencrypt a file, you need to have the proper utility software available. To control how your files are treated, you need to learn what features are in the mail software you use. The safest universal way to ship text files and messages is as ASCII rather than formatted text. Most word processors will support saving of documents into straight text, which then allows you to incorporate them smoothly into mail messages. If you do get a file you need to decode, there are various shareware utilities to assist in this (see chapter 8).

2.15

How do I know to whom I'm talking?

The e-mail address of the sender is pretty much your only clue. That's why it's courteous to include a signature, or to provide a complete spelling of the name which the account represents. Some people enjoy the anonymity the 'net can offer, so not all folks will comply with this netiquette advice.

2.16

How do I get one of those fancy signatures?

This is a feature of your mail package. Most software will support the use of a signature. Some software will support more than one signature—for example, a formal and an informal one. Recognizing that space in one's in-box is not infinite, it's polite to be reasonable in the length of a signature. It's also polite to identify yourself clearly on the network by providing your name, title, and several means of communicating with you (see figure 2.12).

****

```
Nancy R. John                          voice: 1-312-996-2716
Assistant University Librarian         fax: 1-312-413-0424
University of Illinois at Chicago      BITNET: U31452@UICVM
Box 8198 m/c 234                       Internet:nancy.john@uic.edu
Chicago IL 60680
```

****

FIGURE 2.12
Signature file from Eudora 2.0.1.

2.17

My correspondents don't always answer my notes. Is there some way I can verify that my message has been received?

Most mail software provides a means to request a return receipt. In some cases, this receipt will be sent when the person actually reads the mail; in other cases, it just means that your message has successfully reached his or her queue of waiting mail (see figures 2.13a and 2.13b).

Troubles with E-mail

The following people HAVE read this memo:

G0094   Valauskas, Edward,GOV   03/21/94 05:31PST

This memo has been routed through a mail gateway to the following people:

JPOLLY@NYSER Delivered to INTERNET# mail system 03/21/94 05:31PST

NOTE : Only delivery to the inbound gateway on another mail system can be confirmed, not delivery to an address.

FIGURE 2.13a
This AppleLink record indicates when a message was passed through an Internet gateway to jpolly@nysernet.org.

This memo has been read by everyone.

The following people HAVE read this memo:

G0094   Valauskas, Edward,GOV   03/20/94 10:35PST
BNARDI   Nardi, Bonnie   03/21/94 13:51PST

FIGURE 2.13b
For mail moving within the confines of the AppleLink system, the AppleLink software provides a more accurate answer to the question, "Who's read this item?"

Troubles with Using LISTSERVs

3

LISTSERV is special software written by Eric Thomas to run on IBM mainframes on BITNET. The software allows the creation of mailing lists and supports the management and distribution of messages and files to the members of the list. A LISTSERV is a group mailing list with a special focus. The list is used to distribute files and electronic mail messages (see figure 3.1). Some LISTSERVs let anyone send messages (see chapter 2) and files, others are restricted to subscribers, and still others are under the control of a moderator or editor who screens postings for their appropriateness. LISTSERVs

```
 Message  Edit  Send  Options  Window  Help
─────────────────────────────────────────────────────────────────────
                    Mail from: Gene D. Lanier     Lines 1 to 19 of 97
                                                        More:    +
Return-Path: <@UICVM.CC.UIC.EDU:owner-alaoif@UICVM.CC.UIC.EDU>
Date:        Wed, 16 Feb 1994 13:24:42 EST
Reply-To:    ifreedom@snoopy.ucis.dal.ca
Sender:      ALAOIF ALA Office for Intellectual Freedom <ALAOIF@UICVM.BITNET>
Comments:    Resent-From: LSLANIER@ECUVM.CIS.ECU.EDU
Comments:    Originally-From: Mike Godwin <mnemonic@eff.org>
From:        "Gene D. Lanier" <LSLANIER@ECUVM.CIS.ECU.EDU>
Subject:     EFF WANTS YOU TO CALL FOR SENATE HEARINGS ON CLIPPER
X-To:        ALAOIF@UICVM.UIC.EDU
To:          Multiple recipients of list ALAOIF <ALAOIF@UICVM.BITNET>

fyi...

Gene D Lanier, Professor & Director of Graduate Studies
East Carolina University
Dept of Library Studies and Educational Technology
─────────────────────────────────────────────────────────────────────
F1 =Help      F2 =Delete   F3 =Quit    F4 =Print    F5 =Reply    F6 =Switch
F7 =Backward  F8 =Forward  F9 =Save    F10=MenuBar  F11=Next     F12=Cancel
====>
```

FIGURE 3.1

Examples of a LISTSERV-distributed message viewed from CMS Rice Mail.

can introduce you to other networkers with your interests and can help you find answers to important questions.

It's easy to join a LISTSERV—just send a message to the LISTSERV software at the machine that hosts the list, telling the software that you want to subscribe. To subscribe to a BITNET LISTSERV, the message is sent to `LISTSERV@<hostname>` with the text `subscribe <listname> <First_Name Last_Name>`. The biggest trouble with LISTSERVs is that an active one can jam up your electronic in-box so hopelessly that you can't do any real work. Here are some other common troubles:

3.01

I subscribed to a list, but I didn't get an acknowledgment.

1. You may not have reached the correct address. Double-check the address of the host machine. How old was the address information? If more than a few weeks, it's best to check. Lists move; names change. Lists were once pretty stable, but the move from mainframes to smaller computers has meant that a number of major lists have found new homes in recent years.

2. Are you sure you sent it to the LISTSERV and not to the list? Sending subscriptions to the list instead of the LISTSERV is one of the most annoying things endured by subscribers to a list. On the other hand, dozens of patient souls will often send you a note explaining how to subscribe to the list without broadcasting your request to the entire list's membership. Of course, others will whine publicly on the list about your ignorance.

3. Did you send the request from your account? If not, the LISTSERV may have used the account you sent the request from. You should always send subscription requests from your own account.

4. Did you make a typo? If you typed `sugbscribe <Your Name>`, the software isn't going to know what you want. You'll need to resubmit your request, or else wait until the human being reviewing the error messages sees your typo and alerts you. In some cases, that person may be able or willing to correct your error, and to add you to the list's subscribers. But it may be several hours, or even days, later. Resubmitting the request yourself is the best

Troubles with Using LISTSERVs

thing to do if you see that you mistyped the command. If you mistyped your name, then you can correct it by using the *register* feature. Send the following mail message or command to the LISTSERV, not the list: `register <Your Correct_Name>`. Do not include the name of any specific list; the *register* command is not list-specific but only applies to BITNET LISTSERVs.

I got an acknowledgment, but I'm not getting any mail.

3.02

You can send a note out to the list to see if there's been any recent activity. You can ask friends or other subscribers (see **3.10**) who subscribe if they have received any mail from the list. Maybe you found one of the few lists with no activity; enjoy it while it lasts.

I'm getting too much mail.

3.03

Now this is more like it. Ask yourself if it's good mail or just a lot of junk. If the latter, take a break from the list by telling the BITNET LISTSERV to set your subscription *NOMAIL*. When you are ready to resume the flood of mail, tell the LISTSERV to reset your subscription *MAIL*. Or maybe the list's output is useful, but there are just too many notes in a day. Then try to set your subscription to the *DIGEST* option (if it is supported by the list), and you'll get one mailing a day with a table of contents and all messages appended.

 This can make for very long files, so be sure you know how to read a long file before you try this option (see **7.10**).

How do I find the name of a list and its host?

3.04

If you know the name and suspect it's a LISTSERV list, you can query the LISTSERV with the command `q <listname>`.

For BITNET LISTSERV lists:

From CMS systems, use the interactive *tell* command and type:

```
tell listserv at <hostname> q <listname>
```

In other systems, send an electronic message addressed to

`listserv@<hostname>` with the text

`query <listname>`

The netwide query is available for BITNET LISTSERVs because BITNET LISTSERV software has a listing available to it of all LISTSERV sites and lists. The LISTSERV software will tell you that it does or doesn't host that list. If the local LIST-SERV doesn't host the list, though, it'll tell you whom it's asking (the LISTSERV software is smart enough to look up the actual host and ask it), and then you'll know the name of the list's `<hostname>`. Or, you can ask the person who told you about the list to give you the particulars. If you don't know the list's name, see **3.05**.

3.05

Is there a list of lists?

A number of subject-based lists are published. Many introductory Internet books (such as those listed in the bibliography) publish selected directories of lists. Peter Rutten, Albert Bayers, and Kelly Maloni's *netguide* (Random House Electronic Publishing) is one printed resource, designed to remind you of *TV Guide*. There's also Edward Hardie and Vivian Neou's *Internet: Mailing Lists* (Prentice-Hall).

But any paper-based directory is fossilized as it's being printed. There's nothing more mercurial than lists. For a more dynamic directory, at least for academic discussion lists, `FTP ksuvxa.kent.edu`. At the prompt for a userid, type `anonymous`. Your password is your `<userid>` on your own computer. Once you're in the computer at Kent State University, type `cd library`. There are 14 files for discussion lists covering everything from anthropology to Yiddish literature. Type `GET <Filename>.<Filetype>` to pick up the files.

A directory of electronic newsletters and journals is stored at the University of Ottawa,

`FTP panda1.uottawa.ca`

Again, at the prompt for a userid, type `anonymous`. Use your `<userid>` as the password. Now that you're in Ottawa, type `cd /pub/religion/`. Then type `get electronic-serials-directory.txt <localfilename>`. If all of this seems confusing, the Association of Research Libraries (ARL) annually publishes the *Directory of Electronic Journals, Newsletters and*

Troubles with Using LISTSERVs

Academic Discussion Lists, a printed snapshot of these digital directories. ARL also puts the *Directory* on diskette.

Finally, there's another master list of lists, kept just for the BITNET LISTSERV community. You can obtain that list by sending (interactively or via e-mail) the command *LIST GLOBAL* to the nearest LISTSERV. (Watch out! It's more than 3,500 lines long.) Type `list global`.

How do I unsubscribe?

3.06

Remember that acknowledgment you received when you subscribed? It told you how to unsubscribe. There are two ways to unsubscribe: Send the command SIGNOFF to the LISTSERV@<hostname>. Or if you are really fed up (or your address is changing), you can send the message SIGNOFF (NETWIDE and the LISTSERV will close out all your subscriptions.

Can I shut off the list while I'm on vacation?

3.07

Sure, and this is a great idea unless you like to have your in-box overflowing when you return. To shut off the mail, send the LISTSERV software (*not* the list) the command SET NOMAIL. To resume mail service, tell the LISTSERV (*not* the list) to SET MAIL. (To review the mail you missed, see **3.12**.)

My replies are going to the sender and I want them to go to the list (or to the list and I want them to go to the sender).

3.08

There are a couple of issues here. First, the person who set up the list made a decision about whether the list or the original sender (or both) is retained in the "from" field in the messages sent out to the list. You can't change that, but noticing which was chosen will help you. To determine where the reply will go, you need to READ the mail header on your outgoing mail BEFORE you send it. This can help you avoid the truly embarrassing situation of sending out a highly personal note to 200 relative strangers. Your mail software may allow you to choose to whom a reply goes with special commands such as REPLY FROM, REPLYTO, and REPLY ALL. To be safest, *never* reply; always begin each note anew with the target addresses.

Also, be kind to your friends. When you forward mail from a list to a friend, get rid of the "list-supplied-to" and "from" fields so that your pals aren't tricked into sending a private reply out to a list (see figure 2.9c).

3.09

I sent a reply to the list that I didn't mean to send. I want to get it back.

Can't do, unless you know someone who can stop the LIST-SERV from distributing its mail. And given the speed of the 'net, such a rescue is a long shot. The best course of action is to learn from the humiliation, practice safer replying (read above), and apologize to anyone whose feelings you hurt. Don't apologize to the whole list, which just compounds the felony. As Miss Manners says, if it's a minor offense, just pretend it didn't happen: "What note? Someone else must have been using my account."

3.10

I want to see who subscribes.

The Digital Hugeness is an open hugeness, so go ahead and look. The LISTSERV software allows you to *REVIEW* a list you subscribe to, and many lists are open to review even if you don't subscribe. *REVIEW* provides subscriber addresses.

3.11

I don't want others to see that I subscribe to the list.

The Digital Hugeness is an open hugeness that believes in freedom of choice, so if you don't want your name generally available to those who might send you junk mail, then keep your subscription *CONCEAL*ed when you subscribe. The command is `set <listname> conceal`.

3.12

I saw a note a couple of months ago. I didn't keep it. Can I get it back?

Sure, IF the list is archived. Many lists keep their own archives. If your list is archived, you can ask the LISTSERV to send you the LOG file for that week or month. That's how you can read mail you missed on vacation. To see if and what archive files are available, ask the LISTSERV to send you the `INDEX <listname>`, and then ask it to `SEND <logfilename>`.

```
Ready; T=0.01/0.03 21:45:30
tell listserv index notis-l
Ready; T=0.01/0.02 21:45:58
RDR FILE 0637 SENT FROM LISTSERV PUN WAS 7998 RECS 0070 CPY  001 N
NOHOLD NOKEEP
  * File "NOTIS-L FILELIST" has been sent to you in Netdata format.
```

FIGURE 3.2a

A query is sent via CMS to the LISTSERV requesting an index for NOTIS-L. The system responds by sending the list of files available (NOTIS-L FILELIST). Note: No <nodename> was needed after `listserv` because NOTIS-L is hosted by the node on which the query was sent.

```
* * * Top of File * * *
*   NOTIS-L FILELIST for LISTSERV@UICVM.
*
*   Archives for list NOTIS-L (NOTIS discussion group list)
*
*  ::::::::::::::::::::::::::::::::::::::::::::::::::::::::::::::::::::::::
*
*   The GET/PUT authorization codes shown with each file entry describe
*   who is authorized to GET or PUT the file:
*
*
*      ALL = Everybody
*      OWN = List owners
*
*  ::::::::::::::::::::::::::::::::::::::::::::::::::::::::::::::::::::::::
*
*   NOTEBOOK archives for the list
*   (Weekly notebook)
*                            rec             last - change
* filename filetype   GET PUT -fm lrecl nrecs  date      time    Remarks
* -------- --------   --- --- --- ----- ----- -------- -------- --------
  NOTIS-L  LOG9307C   ALL OWN V      80   636 93/07/21 15:42:48 Started on Thu,
  NOTIS-L  LOG9307D   ALL OWN V      79   829 93/07/28 17:01:26 Started on Thu,
  NOTIS-L  LOG9307E   ALL OWN V      79   734 93/07/31 14:19:39 Started on Thu,
  NOTIS-L  LOG9308A   ALL OWN V      80  2598 93/08/06 16:40:53 Started on Sun,
  NOTIS-L  LOG9401D   ALL OWN V      80  1785 94/01/28 15:04:40 Started on Fri,
  NOTIS-L  LOG9401E   ALL OWN V      78   350 94/01/31 16:03:26 Started on Sat,
  NOTIS-L  LOG9402A   ALL OWN V      80  1294 94/02/07 17:58:08 Started on Tue,
  NOTIS-L  LOG9402B   ALL OWN V      80  1159 94/02/14 15:26:04 Started on Tue,
  NOTIS-L  LOG9402C   ALL OWN V      80  1557 94/02/21 17:49:50 Started on Tue,
  NOTIS-L  LOG9402D   ALL OWN V      80  1979 94/02/28 15:17:58 Started on Tue,
  NOTIS-L  LOG9403A   ALL OWN V      83  1671 94/03/07 15:28:44 Started on Tue,
  NOTIS-L  LOG9403B   ALL OWN V      86   874 94/03/14 15:12:08 Started on Tue,
  NOTIS-L  LOG9403C   ALL OWN V      80   896 94/03/21 16:24:35 Started on Tue,
  NOTIS-L  LOG9403D   ALL OWN V      78    70 94/03/22 17:51:48 Started on Tue,
* * * End of File * * *

====> tell listserv get notis-l log9403D
```

FIGURE 3.2b

The list of archived files available from NOTIS-L with the command requesting one particular file typed on the CMS command line.

```
NOTIS-L  LOG9403D A1  V 80  Trunc=80 Size=70 Line=35 Col=1 Alt=0

==========================================================================
Date:          Tue, 22 Mar 1994 15:25:51 -0600
Reply-To:      NOTIS discussion group list <NOTIS-L@UICVM.BITNET>
Sender:        NOTIS discussion group list <NOTIS-L@UICVM.BITNET>
From:          BARBARA L BAUGHMAN <baughman@UTDALLAS.EDU>
Subject:       Re: OPAC Statistics using SAS
In-Reply-To:   <94Mar21.095949cst.13897@utdallas.edu>

In response to Keith, I am sending something called OPACFILE to
NOTISPRO.  It has the SAS format of the LPCLOGF file.  From there you
should be able to write SAS programs to work with it.

Babs Baughman
TECH1
University of Texas at Dallas
(214) 690-2157
BAUGHMAN@UTDALLAS.EDU
VSE/SP 4.1.2  CICS 1.7
LMS 5.1.1    GTO 3.1
====>
```

FIGURE 3.2c
A message retrieved from the NOTIS-L archive.

If you really only want one particular note, and the list is archived, you may be able to run a database search against the archive to find that note. To find out how to search the archives, send the command `info database` to the LISTSERV.

```
Connecting to LISTSERV@UICVM, please be patient.

Welcome to LISTSERV@UICVM - Release 1.7f (FIX17F2), backbone server.
CPU model 3090, DASD model 3390.

Enter command, or "QUIT" to exit:
search subject infoshare in notis-l

Search started...
--> Database NOTIS-L, 99 hits.

Enter command, or "QUIT" to exit:
help

Basic commands are:
  Select <search-rules> <IN db-list> <WHERE specs> <date-specs>
  Index
  Print  <portion-name> <OF items-list><, portion-name <OF...>>
  SENDback any-command (sends you the output as a file)
For more information, refer to the "Revised LISTSERV: Database
Functions"
(document number U01-012), available through an "INFO DATABASE" command.

Enter command, or "QUIT" to exit:
send index

RDR FILE 0646 SENT FROM LISTSERV PUN WAS 8831 RECS 0076 CPY  001 N
NOHOLD NOKEEP
* File "DATABASE OUTPUT" has been sent to you in Netdata format.

Enter command, or "QUIT" to exit:
quit

Session has been cancelled.

Ready; T=0.18/0.40 22:07:45
```

FIGURE 3.3a

Log of a keyword (infoshare) search of the archive of NOTIS-L using the CMS LISTSERV search program LDBASE.
The log shows the search of the file, and the request for a copy of the index to be sent to the searcher. Boldface in this
example marks the user's input.

```
 DATABASE OUTPUT    A1   V 80   Trunc=80 Size=102 Line=10 Col=1 Alt=0

 > index
 Item #    Date    Time   Recs    Subject
 ------    ----    ----   ----    -------
 000028 93/07/08 14:55    24    Infoshare and CD-ROM access
 000029 93/07/08 21:37    51    Re: Infoshare and CD-ROM access
 000031 93/07/09 08:16    71    Re: Infoshare and CD-ROM access
 000032 93/07/09 08:14    16    Re: Infoshare and CD-ROM access
 000034 93/07/09 09:04    21    Re: Infoshare and CD-ROM access
 000040 93/07/10 16:29    36    Re: Infoshare and CD-ROM access
 000042 93/07/12 09:02    13    Re: Infoshare and CD-ROM access
 000043 93/07/12 11:17    13    CD-ROMS on Infoshare
 000049 93/07/13 10:17    13    Infoshare
 000069 93/07/14 14:55    23    InfoShare TAG
 000072 93/07/14 14:46    16    InfoShare TAG
 000075 93/07/15 10:35    25    Re: InfoShare TAG
 000084 93/07/16 12:57    29    Infoshare and OPAC displays
 000085 93/07/16 14:02    42    Re: Infoshare and OPAC displays
 000091 93/07/20 00:44    58    InfoShare and CD-ROMs
 000094 93/07/21 15:41    13    Capturing of patron use statistics in
 MDAS/INFOSha

 ====>
```

FIGURE 3.3b
The copy of the index sent to the searcher as a result of the LDBASE search.

Finally, a lot of lists are archived and available via various network tools (Internet Gopher, WAIS, Mosaic).

3.13

I'm getting two copies of every posting to the list.

This usually means—surprise—that you have two subscriptions. Maybe the LISTSERV has two versions of your address. You may have subscribed from different accounts, resulting in multiple subscriptions. Or maybe the list's owner subscribed you and made a mistake. The solution is simple: signoff one of them. The other possibility is that some list software can hit a snag and lose its place sending mail, and so it sends out a second (or multiple) round of mail (sort of a "virtual hiccup"), but this is rare, and would not account for consistent duplicate mailings.

Troubles with Using LISTSERVs

Whenever I send a note to the list, I don't get a copy of it in my mail from the list.

3.14

Whether or not you receive a copy of your note back depends on the settings governing your subscription. Some lists are set to send a copy of your note back to you.

If you'd like to set your subscription up so that you'll always get a copy of your mail to the list, then let the LIST-SERV know to `set <listname> repro` for your subscription.

I'm getting mail from a list. When I try to change my subscription, the LISTSERV doesn't know me. When I try to send it mail, it says I'm not subscribed. Yet I keep getting mail.

3.15

Sounds like your address changed. Did you signoff from the account you subscribed from originally and then resubscribe from your new address? If you can no longer send from that account, send a message to `<listname>-owner@<hostname>` asking the list's owner to remove or change your address from the list. Be sure to include your former address. That way the owner can find your subscription and remove it so you don't get duplicates if you are staying subscribed under your new address.

You can also send a `review` command (see **3.10**) to find out the address of the owner of the list, and then ask the owner to make the change. Or, in total desperation, you can send a note to the postmaster at the node hosting the list (`postmast@<hostname>`).

I want to know about new lists.

3.16

There's a list! (`NEW-LIST@NDSUVM1`)

Troubles with Owning LISTSERV Lists

List managers support global discussion and collaboration over the Internet and the distribution of materials in electronic formats. It's easy to own a LISTSERV list. That's when the fun begins. The biggest trouble with LISTSERV lists is that an active one can clog up your electronic in-box so hopelessly that you can't do anything. Here are some other common troubles.

I want to start a list. What do I have to do?

1. First, check to make sure the list you want to start doesn't already exist. With more than 3,500 lists already in business and many thousands more Usenet newsgroups, you may be trying to reinvent the wheel (see **3.05**). Also, check with NEW-LIST@NDSUVM1 where new lists are announced and "Does anybody know?" queries are answered.

2. Find a site with the LISTSERV software installed (by looking in the global list and seeing which sites have lists) and ask them to host the list. The original LISTSERV software resides on mainframes on BITNET.

Many Internet sites run various Unix LISTSERV-type software. CREN, BITNET's successor, has acquired the rights to the Unix-TCP/IP list management and file distribution software developed by Anastasios Kotsikonas and known as *ListProcessor* and *ListProc*, currently in use at more than 300 sites throughout the world to manage over 4,500 electronic mailing lists. A release toward the end of 1994 is expected to include enhancements not available in the first release, e.g., the capability of hierarchically distributing list postings. Version 6.0c (the current version) of *ListProc* is to remain available at no cost for noncommercial use. CREN also expects to develop Mac- and Windows-based list management clients to facilitate the use of the server for list subscription, signing off, information requests, and other list management functions required of list owners and list initiators.

4.02

I tried to unsubscribe someone and it didn't work.

First, list owners *add* and *delete* subscribers. Subscribers *subscribe* and *signoff* (themselves). List owners can only *signoff* themselves. Subscribers cannot *add* or *delete* themselves or others.

Assuming that you were using the correct command and syntax, the most likely explanation is that the person is subscribed under a different address than the one you used to try to *delete* them from the list of subscribers. Given the dynamic nature of addresses over the past several years, it's no small wonder. The user's postmaster has probably put into place the necessary information so that mail gets forwarded to their current address, but the person has probably long since forgotten that he subscribed under an older or different account. Of course, one legitimate reason why you cannot find the person in the list is that the person may not have subscribed to the list directly. Instead, the subscriber may be receiving the mailings from an intermediary distribution list (that is subscribed to your list) that offers its own subscriptions. If this is the case, the subscriber will need to contact the owner of the intermediary distribution service.

4.03

I keep getting reports of mail not being delivered to a particular node or several nodes.

Most list management software and mailers work together to keep trying to deliver the mail while there's an outage. Often you'll be notified that there is an outage but that the software is trying to deliver the mail, so that you can alert your subscribers to the situation. But some of the messages mean that there is a problem and that you need to correct a bad address, or remove someone from the subscription list.

```
Return-Path: <LISTSERV@UICVM.CC.UIC.EDU>
Received: from UICVM.UIC.EDU (NJE origin LISTSERV@UICVM) by UICVM.CC.UIC.EDU
(LMail V1.2a/1.8a) with BSMTP id 0405; Wed, 23 Mar 1994 15:21:54 -0600
Date:   Wed, 23 Mar 1994 15:21:54 -0600
From:   BITNET list server at UICVM (1.7f) <LISTSERV@UICVM.UIC.EDU>
Subject:       ALA-WO: error report from USCN
To:     ALAWASH@ALAWASH.ORG,
Nancy John <U31452@UICVM.BITNET>
X-LSV-ListID: None

The enclosed mail file, found in the ALA-WO reader and shown under the spoolid 7113 in
the console log, has been identified as a possible delivery error notice for the
following reason: "Sender:", "From:" or "Reply-To:" field pointing to the list has
been found in mail body.

---------------------- Message in error (249 lines) ------------------------
Message-ID: <940323162214.00F1A040.FIEH.UG@USCN> Date: 23 Mar 94 16:22:14 EST
From: Name server <Server@USCN>
To: <ALA-WO@UICVM.BITNET>
Subject: Unknown addresses
```

The following address is unknown to the name server:

abcdefg@USCN

```
+-------------------------------+
: Your original message follows :
+-------------------------------+

Received: from UGA (MAILER) by USCN for <abcdefg@USCN> via BITNet
with NJF id ALA-WO; 23 Mar 94 16:20:54 EST
Return-Path: <@UGA.CC.UGA.EDU:owner-ala-wo@UICVM.UIC.EDU>
Received: from UGA.CC.UGA.EDU (NJE origin LISTSERV@UGA) by UGA.CC.UGA.EDU
(LMail V1.1d/1.7f) with BSMTP id 1689; Wed, 23 Mar 1994 16:18:44 -0500
Date:   Wed, 23 Mar 1994 16:09:14 -0500
Reply-To:      ALA Washington Office Update <ALA-WO@UICVM.BITNET>
Sender:        ALA Washington Office Update <ALA-WO@UICVM.BITNET>
From:   ALA Washington Office <alawash@alawash.org>
Subject:       ALAWON, Vol. 3, No. 14
X-To:   ala-wo@uicvm.uic.edu
To:     Multiple recipients of list ALA-WO <ALA-WO@UICVM.BITNET>
```

FIGURE 4.1

Message from a mailer indicating that an address on the list is no longer valid. The list owner will need to unsubscribe or delete this person.

4.04

Can I shut off the list while I'm on vacation?

Not unless you want to anger your subscribers. Of course, if the list is a one-way distribution of information (i.e., edited list) and not a free-for-all chat list, you can shut down for a while. But courtesy suggests that you warn your readers that there won't be any messages for a while (so they don't think there's something wrong with their domains and start troubleshooting from their ends).

4.05

Replies are going to the sender and I want them to go to the list (or they are going to the list and I want them to go to the sender).

LISTSERV documentation is a bit sparse, so perseverance is important in determining how to do something. The list management software allows you to prescribe whether the list, the sender, or both go into the reply-to field of the messages that are sent out from the list.

```
*
*    NOTIS discussion group list
*
*    Confidential=    No
*    Review=          Public
*    Subscription=    Open
*    Send=            Public
*    Notify=          No
*     Reply-to=               List,Respect
*    Files=           No
*    Validate=        Store Only
*    Ack=             No
*    Formcheck=       Yes
*    Mail-via=        Dist2
*    Notebook=        Yes,L,Weekly,Public
*
*
*    Owner=           U31452@UICVM
*    Errors-To=       U31452@UICVM
*
```

FIGURE 4.2
Header of a VM/CMS LISTSERV list showing the various settings, including the setting that determines which address goes in the replyto field.

Troubles with Owning LISTSERV Lists

**I sent a reply to the list that I didn't mean to send.
I want to get it back.**

Unless the server is slow and you know someone with the power to purge the mail to it, there's nothing you can do. As a list owner, you may have powers that will allow you to do some things accidentally that you don't want to do. For example, if a subscriber sends a file to a moderated list, it'll bounce to the moderator. If you, as the moderator or owner, send a file to the list by accident, it will get distributed to all the subscribers!

Troubles with News Readers 5

News reading is a popular 'net pastime. The news can come from a variety of sources, including a wire service, a major U.S. newspaper, a service providing transcripts of television and radio news and talk programs, or one of the network's lists or newsgroups where networkers talk to each other. Usenet news is a collection of dynamic files called "newsgroups," where people read and post their highly personal, informative, and outrageous points of view.

These services can be made available via special servers based on the Network News Transfer Protocol (NNTP). Readers connect to the server with a news reader client. Most clients are available as shareware or freeware and allow reading, responding (posting), saving, printing, searching, and managing your access to as many newsgroups as you care to read. The biggest trouble with reading news this way is finding the time to keep up with it. A news reader can't help you find the time, but a good one can help you manage it so your news reading time is productive, spent reading groups you are interested in and viewing them in an orderly fashion.

What's the difference between LISTSERVs and Usenet news? Well, the obvious one is that LISTSERV grew up in the BITNET world, and Usenet in the Unix world. But things are not that simple anymore. LISTSERVs distribute electronic mail messages to a fixed list of subscriber recipients. Distribution is via SMTP—Simple Mail Transfer Protocol. The messages are read with electronic mail software. Newsgroups are read with news reader software. The news reader software connects to NNTP (Network News Transfer Protocol) servers and downloads information about new postings for those groups to which you have told your software you are a subscriber. Your news software manages your reading.

I have a news reader. Where do I connect?

Most Internet service providers will give you at least some access to news (see figure 5.1). To some extent you get what you pay for in the news arena: for free, you get local networkers talking to other local networkers. Access to the global network news arena can be free, or some services charge by the group or message, or by the hour of reading. Serious—or at least mainstream—news is licensed and only available to those registered to read it.

News reader software may come with suggested servers. These should be your first try. Some Internet sites will allow outside readers. In order to establish a local Usenet server, you need to arrange with an existing site to get a feed of news from them.

```
              ** N E T N E W S   A R T I C L E   M E N U **
Newsgroup soc.libraries.talk - 23 articles - 23 active
Cmd   Userid    Node      Posted   Size  Subject
      EVANS     DEAKIN    03/14/94   41  Re: link indexes first and bidirectional
      LMITTEN   VMS       03/14/94   62  Job opening
      NORING    NETCOM    03/15/94   79  Now Available! The Hypertext "The Devil's
      SABAPATT  NEWTON    03/15/94   37  Effect Of Cellular Phones On Driving
      NORING    NETCOM    03/15/94   72  A Question to Librarians About Electronic
      SOBHANI   DOVE      03/16/94   23  Children's Software.
      YSLIZAK   NYX       03/16/94   26  THANKS! Re: Fax no of a publisher
      RHELLIS   MORGAN    03/16/94   17  re: FirstSearch
      RHELLIS   MORGAN    03/16/94   58  Re: info wanted on library info systems
      TSG045    DELPHI    03/16/94   22  Free material
      KADIE     EFF       03/16/94  147  [UCB] New information management school a
      GLENWOOD  SUPERBOW  03/17/94   38  Library Management Programme
      CBS       GPU       03/17/94   60  Re: info wanted on library info systems
      LEHMANN   RS4       03/17/94   29  help internet addresses
      DSMITH    JULIAN    03/17/94   24  Old Books, Modern Prices?
      HISCRP    LEONIS    03/18/94   34  copyright
  1=Help       2=Refresh    3=Quit       4=In/Xclude  5=NextGroup  6=?
  7=Backward   8=Forward    9=MarkAll   10=Mark/Unmk 11=Display   12=Cursor
 13=Ignore    14=SortSubj  15=QuitAll   16=SetPFK    17=PrevGroup 18=SortCol
 19=BackHalf  20=ForwHalf  21=SeePFKeys 22=AltView   23=AllArts   24=NoRe:
====>
```

FIGURE 5.1

Pennsylvania State University's NETNEWS software server/reader for VM/CMS systems viewing the Usenet newsgroup `soc.libraries.talk`.

Now that I'm connected, how do I post?

First, use common sense. The Usenet code of behavior is a good one:

1. Follow the newsgroup for a few weeks before posting anything to it. Get familiar with the language, style, and level of expertise expected of those who post to the group.

2. Before you post, check the archives, other files, and any local resources to see if the question has been answered already.

3. Post your question to the appropriate newsgroup.

4. Be as brief as possible, but include all the pertinent facts available to you.

5. Include a short, descriptive subject line relating to your posting.

Ready? Okay, then you'll discover that your reader software has the ability to do a *netpost* (the posting of a message to the network). It's very similar to sending <u>e-mail</u> or to participating in a <u>LISTSERV</u>, except that you don't receive the postings personally; you read them off the server. An article's distribution is determined by the group it is posted to (for an example of the *netpost* command, see figure 5.2). You can limit your article's distribution by adding a "Distribution:"

```
U31452    NETPOST   A1   V 80   Trunc=80 Size=2 Line=2 Col=1 Alt=0


* * * Top of File * * *
 Newsgroups:
 Subject:
 Distribution:
* * * End of File * * *


1=Help   2=Choose group   3=Quit
====>
```

FIGURE 5.2a

Example of the netpost screen with `Distribution:` line added as displayed in VM/CMS using Pennsylvania State University's NETNEWS software. Using the option `2=Choose group`(using the F2 key) brings up a list of groups and their brief descriptions as follows in figure 5.2b.

Troubles with News Readers

line in the article header and indicate one of the following: world or net (entire network); usa (United States); or bit (BITNET sites).

```
GROUP NAME                              DESCRIPTION

bit.listserv.eltonjohn
bit.listserv.emedch-l                   Early Medieval China.
bit.listserv.emtex
bit.listserv.emusic-l                   Electronic Music Discussion List.
bit.listserv.endnote                    Bibsoft Endnote Discussions.
bit.listserv.envbeh-l                   Forum on Environment and Human Behavior.
bit.listserv.esri-l
bit.listserv.ethics-l                   Discussion of Ethics in Computing.
bit.listserv.euearn-l                   Computers in Eastern Europe.
bit.listserv.exlibris                   Rare Books and Special Collections Forum.
bit.listserv.feline-l                   Cats.
bit.listserv.feminist                   ALA Feminist Task Force Discussion Group.
bit.listserv.film-l                     Film making and reviews List.
bit.listserv.fnord-l                    New Ways of Thinking List.
bit.listserv.forkni-l                   Forever Knight TV Show.
bit.listserv.frac-l                     FRACTAL Discussion List.
bit.listserv.free-l                     Fathers Rights and Equality Discussions.
bit.listserv.games-l                    Computer Games List.
bit.listserv.gaynet                     GayNet Discussion List. (Moderated)
bit.listserv.gddm-l                     The GDDM Discussion List.
      Place cursor by group name and press PF11.

====>
```

FIGURE 5.2b
To select a group and have it automatically added to the Newsgroup: line, place the computer's cursor next to the name of the group and hit the F11 key.

5.03

There are several groups I think would be interested in my posting. Must I retype it/resubmit it for each one?

No. The feature you need is the ability to cross-post. Most news readers will support this. *But please* don't broadcast a posting to lots of groups with marginal interest in your query or information (see figure 5.3). Most networkers read more than one group. If you think there will be people on two groups interested in the posting, remember that if you read both groups, so do many others. Cross-posting is, unfortunately, easy. Just type the names of the newsgroups or discussion lists into the address field, input the message, and send.

Troubles with News Readers

```
U31452    NETPOST   A1   V 80   Trunc=80 Size=2 Line=2 Col=1 Alt=0
```

```
* * * Top of File * * *
 Newsgroups: pacs-l@uhupvm1 libadmin@ubvm comp.info.systems.gopher
 Subject: Posting on gopher servers by library users

I am interested in finding out what others are doing about providing public
access to *posting* information on a public gopher server in a library.
Do you place limits on what can be posted? Its length? The subject matter?
Do you let individuals post the documents themselves? Do you use a special
program to do it automatically? Do you screen postings?

Please respond to me and I will summarize for the lists.

Nancy John, Asst. University Librarian
University of Illinois at Chicago
* * * End of File * * *
1=Help  2=Choose group   3=Quit
====>
```

FIGURE 5.3
This posting will be cross-posted to three newsgroups.

Can I post binary files to newsgroups?

5.04

Technically you can do this, but you won't win any friends among the readership. You'll probably generate a lot of complaints or at least some lively discussion, *except* for the group of newsgroups with the word BINARIES in their names. These folks will welcome your binary file.

Now that I'm connected, how do I reply?

5.05

First, be polite (see **5.02**). There are two kinds of replies. There are follow-ups that go to the entire readership (or group) and there are replies that go as private messages to the author of the original posting as regular electronic mail. Most news reader software supports both, or else has an interface to your local e-mail software for private replies. In addition, there are special features that can shape what the "reply" will look like. For example, in the Unix reader program *trn* : f is a follow-up without the original text; F is a follow-up with the original text; r is a reply to the author without the original text; R is a reply to the author with the original text. Note: while F and R include the complete original text, you should still consider editing it down to its essential parts (see figure 5.4).

```
 ARTICLE   NETNEWS   A1   V 511   Trunc=511 Size=25 Line=2 Col=1 Alt=0
Newsgroup(s): rec.pets.cats                    This article marked on exit
From: baukusl@cranium.com.msu.edu (Lori Baukus)
Subject: Re: Cat eats plants
Date: Sun, 20 Mar 1994 19:46:43 GMT

In article <BEMUS.94Mar18094129@brio.mit.edu> bemus@brio.mit.edu (Sally C. Santi
ago) writes:
>From: bemus@brio.mit.edu (Sally C. Santiago)
>Subject: Cat eats plants
>Date: 18 Mar 1994 14:41:29 GMT

>You might try the following.  Go out in the back yard and dig up a piece of
>it and bring it in the house.

WARNING!  WARNING!

We got a wonderful bug infestation this way!  Now I stick to potting soil and
seeds from scratch!
* * * End of File * * *
  1=Help        2=Followup    3=Quit        4=Save        5=Reply       6=?
  7=Backward    8=Forward     9=Mark/Unmk 10=PrevArt    11=NextArt    12=Cursor
====>
```

FIGURE 5.4a
Note inclusion of the essential part of the original note and the use of the word WARNING! to catch the attention of the reader. Pressing the F2 key results in the following NETPOST (figure 5.4b) being created for posting a follow-up to the newsgroup. Pressing F5 would reply directly to the author of this note and no posting would be made to the newsgroup.

```
 U31452    NETPOST   A1   V 80   Trunc=80 Size=22 Line=9 Col=1 Alt=0
Date: Sun, 20 Mar 1994 18:34:58 CST
From: Nancy John <U31452@uicvm.uic.edu>
Message-ID: <94079.183458U31452@uicvm.uic.edu>
Newsgroups: rec.pets.cats
Subject: Re: Cat eats plants
References: <BEMUS.94Mar18094129@brio.mit.edu>
 <baukus1.127.2D8CA823@cranium.com.msu.edu>




Please read HELP NETNEWS ETIQUETTE before posting.

 1=Help        2=Lineadd    3=Quit      4=SInput    5=Post      6=?
 7=Backward    8=Forward    9=Original 10=Sign     11=Split    12=Cursor
====> * * * Input Zone * * *
```

FIGURE 5.4b
Example of a posting and the form for posting a follow-up in Penn State's NETNEWS as viewed under VM/CMS.

There are many topics under discussion in a news group. Is there a way to follow a single topic?

5.06

That depends. Some news readers will group messages by subject or thread (see figure 5.5). The ability of the software to do this depends on whether the people talking on the group are posting their replies and responses as follow-ups to the original topic of conversation, or as new postings. If they post replies as new postings, then it can be difficult for the computer to connect them to the ongoing discussion.

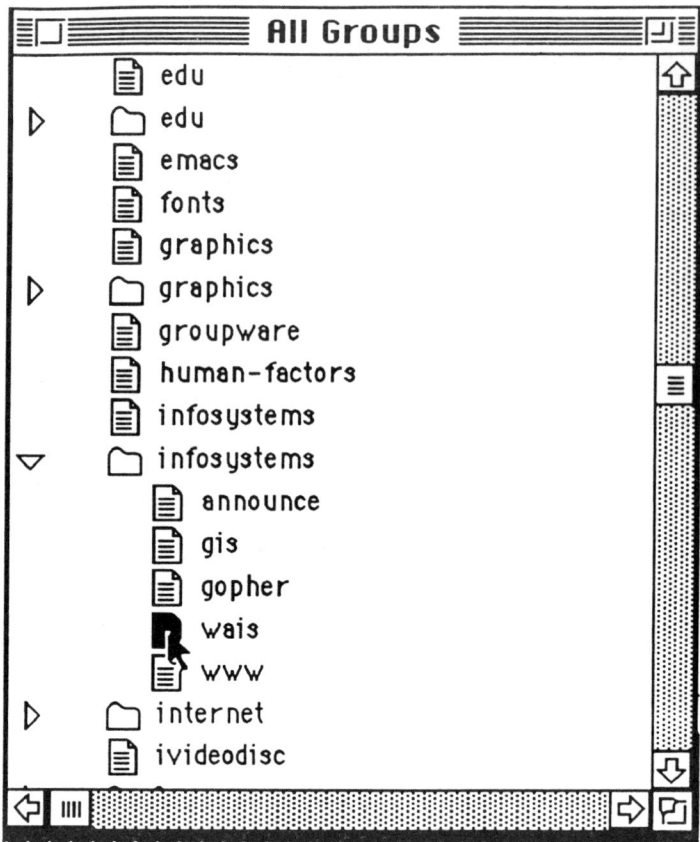

FIGURE 5.5a

Example of Nuntius 1.1.3 (a Macintosh news reader by Peter Speck) window showing all files available from the NNTP server at uicvm.uic.edu.

Troubles with News Readers

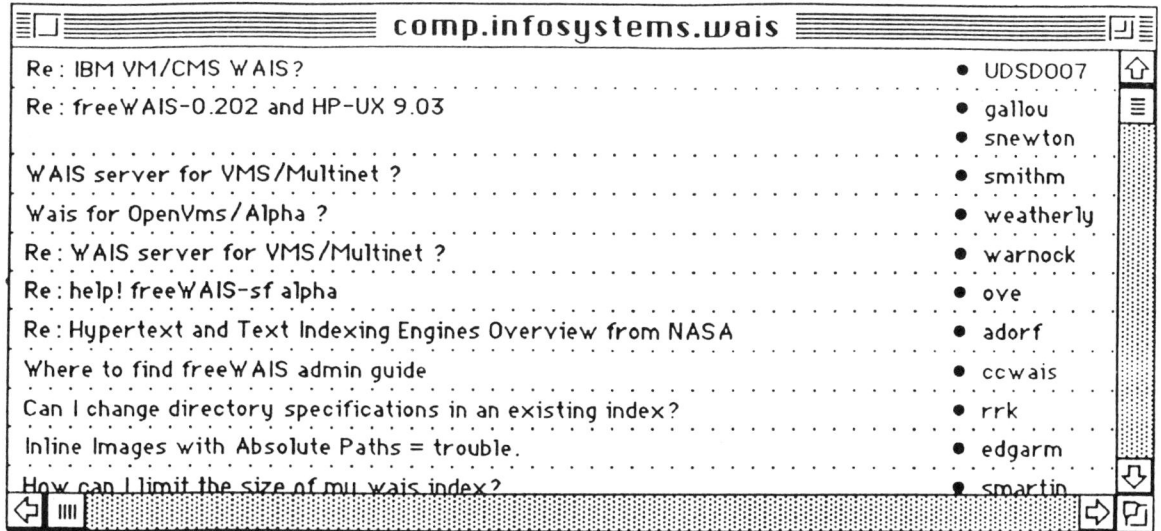

FIGURE 5.5b

This Nuntius window contains part of the list of unread articles posted to the newsgroup `comp.infosystems.wais`.

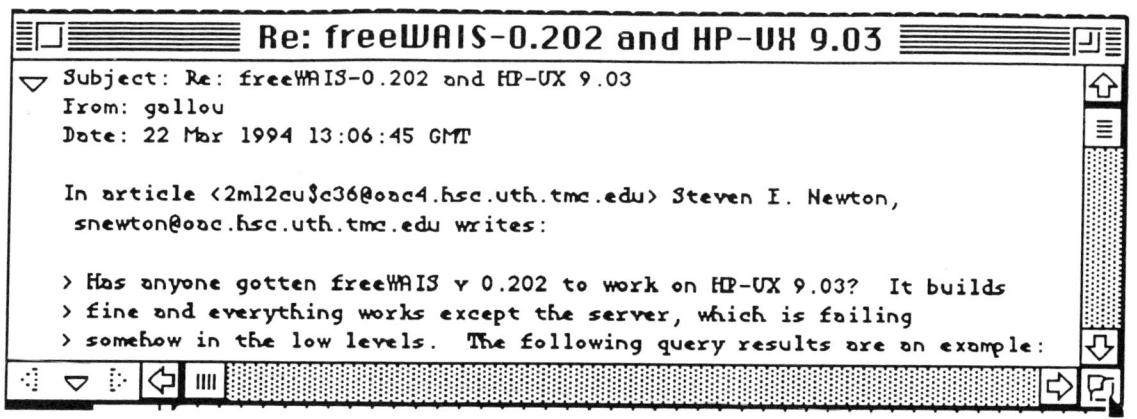

FIGURE 5.5c

This Nuntius window displays two messages posted to the same thread.

Yesterday I saw a posting I wanted to read, but I didn't have time. Today, I can't find it. Why did it disappear?

The most likely explanation is that your news reader is set to show you only items you haven't seen before (see figure 5.6). Since you saw the posting, the news reader remembered and is blocking it from being displayed to you. Most readers have a feature to override the filtering and to display all messages (threads). A second explanation is that your server keeps only x amount of files around—x varies by policy and space available. So the administrator of the server could have purged that day's postings to make room for newer ones. Finally, each message on Usenet should have an expiration date, and the messages you saw may have expired.

```
            ** N E T N E W S   A R T I C L E   M E N U **
Newsgroup jrnl.npr.all-things-considered - 178 articles - 178 active
Cmd  Userid    Node      Posted    Size   Subject
     JOURNAL. BOBJ       03/25/94  160    Hebron gun Battle Kills Five, Endangers P
     JOURNAL. BOBJ       03/25/94  195    Embryo Research Begs Many Ethical, Moral
     JOURNAL. BOBJ       03/25/94  272    [1/2] A Comprehensive Report on the White
     JOURNAL. BOBJ       03/26/94   51    No subject
     JOURNAL. BOBJ       03/26/94  124    NFL Goes Through Kickoff Reform
     JOURNAL. BOBJ       03/26/94  116    Philip Morris Files Suit Against ABC
     JOURNAL. BOBJ       03/26/94  136    More Americans Finding Whitewater Impedin
     JOURNAL. BOBJ       03/26/94  201    Clinton Pledges Cooperation, Disclosure o
     JOURNAL. BOBJ       03/26/94  154    Harsh Winter on East Coast Costing Big Bu
     JOURNAL. BOBJ       03/26/94   50    [2/2] Hebron a City Divided
     JOURNAL. BOBJ       03/26/94  134    Israel and PLO Make Progress in Cairo Tal
     JOURNAL. BOBJ       03/26/94   98    Listeners Sound Off on Pinkwater, Politic
     JOURNAL. BOBJ       03/26/94  204    Taft High School Nixes Alternate Bell Sch
*    JOURNAL.  BOBJ  03/26/94   125    *Rumors of Yeltsin's Ill Health Draw Specu
     JOURNAL. BOBJ       03/26/94  272    [1/2] Hebron a City Divided
     JOURNAL. BOBJ       03/26/94  183    Assassination in Mexico Alters Political
```

FIGURE 5.6a

Reading a transcript of a broadcast on National Public Radio's "All Things Considered" invokes a "mark" in the news reader, signaled by an asterisk.

```
            ** N E T N E W S   N E W S G R O U P   M E N U **
3211 non-empty newsgroups - 2818 active
Cmd  Articles(Read) Newsgroup
         94          jrnl.npr.weekend-edition
        184          jrnl.npr.morning-edition
*        178(1)        jrnl.npr.all-things-considered
        121          jrnl.misc
          1          jrnl.cnn.your-money
         14          jrnl.cnn.special-assignment
         58          jrnl.cnn.sonya
         17          jrnl.cnn.showbiz-today
          2          jrnl.cnn.science-and-technology-week
          6          jrnl.cnn.reliable-sources
          2          jrnl.cnn.pinnacle
          4          jrnl.cnn.newsmaker-saturday
        165          jrnl.cnn.news
         71          jrnl.cnn.montel_williams
          2          jrnl.cnn.moneyweek
         19          jrnl.cnn.moneyline
```

FIGURE 5.6b

The news reader keeps track that the user has examined one of 178 articles under the option "All Things Considered."

```
            ** N E T N E W S   A R T I C L E   M E N U **
Newsgroup jrnl.npr.all-things-considered - 178 articles - 177 active
Cmd  Userid   Node    Posted    Size   Subject
     JOURNAL. BOBJ    03/25/94   107   Tensions, Suspicion High on Both Sides of
     JOURNAL. BOBJ    03/25/94   160   Hebron gun Battle Kills Five, Endangers P
     JOURNAL. BOBJ    03/25/94   195   Embryo Research Begs Many Ethical, Moral
     JOURNAL. BOBJ    03/25/94   272   [1/2] A Comprehensive Report on the White
     JOURNAL. BOBJ    03/26/94    50   [2/2] Hebron a City Divided
     JOURNAL. BOBJ    03/26/94   134   Israel and PLO Make Progress in Cairo Tal
     JOURNAL. BOBJ    03/26/94    98   Listeners Sound Off on Pinkwater, Politic
     JOURNAL. BOBJ    03/26/94   204   Taft High School Nixes Alternate Bell Sch
     JOURNAL. BOBJ    03/26/94   272   [1/2] Hebron a City Divided
     JOURNAL. BOBJ    03/26/94   183   Assassination in Mexico Alters Political
 1=Help       2=Refresh    3=Quit       4=In/Xclude  5=NextGroup  6=?
 7=Backward   8=Forward    9=MarkAll   10=Mark/Unmk 11=Display   12=Cursor
13=Ignore    14=SortSubj  15=QuitAll   16=SetPFK    17=PrevGroup 18=SortCol
19=BackHalf  20=ForwHalf  21=SeePFKeys 22=AltView   23=AllArts   24=NoRe:
```

FIGURE 5.6c

Returning to "All Things Considered," the news reader no longer displays the article read and marked on an earlier visit. Articles can be marked or unmarked in this news reader by the F10 key.

You'll need to try an archive to locate the message. One of the Internet search tools (veronica, WAIS, or archie) can usually help you locate the backfile of the group.

I posted a message to a newsgroup and it hasn't shown up.

There are a number of possibilities.

1. Your posting is in a queue to be posted.

2. It has been posted, but your reader software filters postings out by matching on your userid. This kind of filtering is a more common occurrence with a personal subscription to a <u>LISTSERV</u> list. If the owner hasn't set the list to `reproduce` the message for the original sender, the originator will not receive a copy of the message in his or her personal mailbox. Note: `repro` can be set by each subscriber as well (see **3.14**).

3. Maybe the group is moderated, and your posting is awaiting review by the moderator.

4. Maybe the group is moderated, and your posting has been rejected by the editor. (Note: You should have received notice of its rejection and why.)

5. Maybe the posting is lost.

How long does it take for a posting to get posted?

It varies from list to list, from newsgroup to newsgroup, based on traffic and the whims of the group's editor for moderated groups. But you can usually expect a posting to appear on the same day. Delays can occur at either end, or in the middle: your mailer is slow sending the posting, their mailer is slow receiving it, theirs is slow posting it, and yours is slow receiving the posted message. It could be that the news server is slow, too.

I want to test out posting with my new news reader. Is there a place I can do that?

Sure. Every day many networkers pick on some poor group and send out a test posting. Don't do this. It's not nice. Groups are for talking about a topic. Don't use them for testing or other personal activities. That's why `alt.test` and `misc.test` in Usenet exist. Send your test posting there. Then go read it.

I posted a message (I've seen it posted), but I haven't heard a thing. What's happening?

5.11

There's no rule that every posting will draw a crowd, even a small one. Some postings will generate a lot of traffic, depending on whose interest you've touched with your message. Many messages, <u>OTOH</u>, create only a few or no replies. Don't give up too quickly, though. Responses may have a lag time of several days as readers wait to see who will answer.

How come I get an acknowledgment of my posting sometimes, but not always?

5.12

It varies from group to group, depending on how the group creator set up the group, and the netiquette of the group's owner. Some lists/groups acknowledge automatically; some don't. Unmoderated newsgroups assume that seeing your posting is your receipt. If you want an acknowledgment sent and the type of group or list supports it, you can always send your posting with a return receipt requested (see **2.16**). Some news server software also will allow you to set your personal distribution options so that you will always receive a receipt.

I saw a response to something, but I didn't see the original request. What happened?

5.13

First, maybe it's lost. Accidents happen. Second, maybe the original hasn't been posted yet. Well, it was posted where the responder is, but maybe not yet where you are. That's because the responder may be closer (electronically speaking) to the poster of the original note and also closer to you than you are to the original poster (electronically speaking). Follow that? This can be attributed to backups in network mail delivery as well.

How can I save a posting?

5.14

The best way is to download the <u>file</u> and save it in your favorite word processor. Be sure to save the name of the sender with the message so that you can attribute correctly or ask permission if you want to quote, re-post, or publish the posting. If you save very many electronic "clippings," you'll find that you'll want to collect them on your hard drive in a special file (subdirectory or folder) to organize these saved treasures.

5.15	**There must be a newsgroup on (you name it— cats, playing bridge, Star Trek . . .). How do I find it?**

Use a network tool, such as <u>veronica</u>, <u>WAIS</u>, <u>WWW</u>, or <u>Gopher</u> (see figure 5.7). There's also the group `news.lists` that provides information on traffic in the most popular newsgroups. You can also inquire about a group by writing to `news.newusers.questions`.

```
Rice CMS Gopher 2.4.2                          cwis.usc.edu
1/7
                     Newsgroups arranged by subject
<document>  Biology, Environmental Science and Agriculture (BESA)
<document>  Engineering, Computer Science and Applied Science (ECSAS)
<document>  Life Sciences (LS)
<document>  Physical Sciences, Earth Sciences and Mathematics (PSESM)
<document>  Clinical Medicine (CM)
<document>  Arts and Humanities (AH)
<document>  Social and Behavioral Sciences (SBS)
```

FIGURE 5.7
Using veronica to search Gophers, it's possible to locate an arrangement of newsgroups by subject.

5.16	**Reading newsgroups is okay, but I really wish I could talk to some people in real time.**

That's a different animal. Internet Relay Chat is one big Internet party line. Get yourself an IRC client and join the continuous chat.

Troubles with News Readers

The names of newsgroups may not be descriptive. Are there published descriptions?

5.17

There are brief descriptions about the newsgroups to explain the focus of a group a bit beyond its name. For Usenet, most groups have FAQs (Frequently Asked Questions) that include a description and also some words about the culture of the group. <u>LISTSERV</u> lists usually don't have FAQs, but at least longer versions of the list names are available on the list of lists. Also there are the numerous guides to the lists, groups, and services on the network (see **3.05**).

I'd like to get to a live news feed from a major news service.

5.18

These are licensed and cost money. Because of that, access to them is restricted to those covered in the licensing agreement. In fact, it may be a violation of the licensing agreement to forward even part of such a posting to someone not eligible to read the group. Major services include Clarinet (wire services), Journal Graphics (transcripts of television and radio), and American Cybercasting (U.S. and international newspapers). Individual news sources have agreements to provide access to their information; America Online has arrangements with a number of U.S. newspapers.

I posted something that made people really angry. Can I get rid of it?

5.19

No, you can't. Consider an apology. Next time review the following *before* you post: commonly accepted rules of etiquette for posting to NETNEWS by Linda Littleton adapted from "A Primer on How to Work with the NETNEWS Community," by Chuq Von Rospach. This document is available from any site running the NETNEWS news reader.

Troubles with Telnet 6

Telnet is the oldest network protocol. The advent of telnet (network terminal emulation) revolutionized traffic on the 'net by creating the first real reason for network travel. Before the telnet protocol, network traffic was not interactive. By allowing for use of a remote system in real time, telnet gave us networkers what we needed—destinations! What could possibly go wrong?

I have an address to telnet to, but when I try nothing happens, or I get messages like "system timeout," "unknown remote host," "host not known," or "host not available."

6.01

Nothing happening is a tricky symptom. Maybe you haven't fully started up the telnet program at your end. If that's not the problem, there are other possibilities: you may have typed the name or address of the remote system incorrectly, the remote system may be down or not active, or the network or the remote system may be filled to the brim with connections with no room for your session. Finally, the remote system may not allow remote login at all or it may allow remote login only from certain addresses.

Is the address numeric? Before the development of the network registries and name servers, many people listed numeric addresses for telnet hosts. It is now generally agreed that names are much more stable and, thus, the preferred address to use. Your local system will use the address to look up in the special server the corresponding up-to-date numeric address for the name. This special server is called a "name server." Use the name, not the number, unless your name server is down and can't look up the name's current numeric address.

I can tell that I'm connected, but I can't do anything.

Terminal incompatibility is a major pitfall in telnetting across the Internet. Just as DOS, Unix, Windows, and Macintosh software are not yet interchangeable, some systems only speak certain protocols. It all depends on the machine from which you are telnetting, the machine to which you are telnetting, and the software in use at both ends of the session.

IBM mainframe systems are inherently dependent on the 3270 terminal architecture, and unless some sort of 3270 protocol converter is between you and one of these systems, your telnet session must speak 3270. Brown University's TN3270 is a popular microcomputer package that emulates a 3270 terminal.

By the same token, certain Unix-based systems have very rigid requirements for the kind of VT100 terminal to which they can talk. This may make it impossible for an IBM mainframe to manage a workable telnet session.

If you are telnetting directly from a microcomputer on the Internet, then successful ubiquitous telnetting will result from choosing a microcomputer program that supports both the VT100 and 3270 terminal emulation via telnet.

The remote system keeps disconnecting me before I can get started.

Assuming that remote login is allowed from wherever you are to the remote system, this is usually a symptom of terminal-host incompatibility or host unavailability. Sometimes a host will offer two addresses—one for 3270 devices and one for VT100 devices—and using an alternate address may help. Waiting until later in the day and trying again may solve the problem.

```
VM TCP/IP Telnet V2R2
Connecting to UHURU.UCHICAGO.EDU 128.135.12.29, port TELNET (23)


Foreign host did not respond within OPEN timeout
Ready; T=0.08/0.13 22:34:10
CMS
```

FIGURE 6.1
Telnet session failed because connection could not be established before timeout was reached.

I have an address, but the system tells me it doesn't exist.

6.04

Telnet software packages are designed to check in with a name server to get current addresses for hostnames. Telnetting by name is supposed to be the safest way. Names are more constant than their attached Internet addresses, which change as gateways and local area networks are reconfigured. When a name can't be translated, it may be that the name server is unavailable, busy, or being updated. If you have the numeric address, see if that works. Finally, you may not have the correct information. Use one of the other Internet tools or a phone call to get the correct name or address.

I get connected, but then I don't know what to do.

6.05

Maybe it's too easy to connect to a system via telnet; you can keep out the riff-raff by keeping the next step obscure. After all, the locals who connect to the system have the documentation and training on site. But assuming that you are connecting to a site that welcomes Internet travelers, there should be some signposts left out for you. Pay attention. Press the return key once or twice, at most—too many presses can put you past the screen that tells you what to do. If nothing happens, try typing the command user to start the login process.

I use the remote system just fine, but I can't get out of it.

6.06

It's as important to know how to get out as how to get in. The opening screen probably gave you some hints, telling you what the *escape* command might be. Jot down this information on a notepad before you begin. For example, in CMS telnet, the characters esc-comma, PA-1, or control-] will work. To quit altogether, type q for quit. Here are some other suggestions to close a remote session: logoff, logof, logout, quit, end, exit, out, stop, bye, and their non-English equivalents (see **1.05**).

The remote system asks for my terminal type, and I can't figure out what mine is.

Usually terminal types are for users who are dialing into the system via telephone line and modem as opposed to connecting over the Internet. Most systems offer a variety of long dead terminal emulations as a vestige of the golden years when dumb terminals outnumbered smart personal computers. But still there are systems that require you to pick a type, and often the only way to discover which one (if any) is right is by hit or miss, working your way through the list. VT100 is the most popular, lowest common denominator, but VT100 emulation can be difficult or impossible for some IBM-3270 systems.

My keyboard doesn't behave the way I expect it to.

This definitely sounds like terminal emulation problems. These can be severe enough to prevent communication. They can also be rather minor annoyances, which you can get used to. For example, if the send key and letter keys work fine, then usually a little playing around can find the combinations to make program-function (pf) keys, numeric keys, the clear and home key, and insert and delete work well enough. For pf-keys, useful experimentation includes trying the escape or control keys with numbers on the keypad or top row of keys on the keyboard.

How do I start a telnet session?

You start up your telnet software—e.g., by clicking on an icon or typing the name of the program. Then you open a session at the particular host by telling your software to connect to a particular address. The telnet command may be as simple as typing `telnet` or `TN3270 <hostname>`, or you may need to start up the telnet software, and then use the `open <hostname>` command.

```
┌─────────────────────────────────────────────────────┐
│  Session name   │uicvm.uic.edu│                      │
│                 └──────────────────────────────────┐ │
│  Window Name    [                                 ] │
│                                                     │
│                 ☐ FTP session (⌘F)                  │
│                 ☐ Serial/SLIP (⌘S)                  │
│                                                     │
│  (Configure)      [ OK ]         (Cancel)           │
└─────────────────────────────────────────────────────┘
```

FIGURE 6.2.
Starting a telnet session using NCSA/BYU Telnet 2.5 for the Macintosh.

How do I stop a telnet session?

6.10

Normal closing of the session should entail logging out of the remote host, and then closing down the telnet session with the command *quit*. Sometimes the remote system isn't very good at telling you how to finish a session. Here are some suggestions to try: `logoff`, `logof`, `logout`, `quit`, `end`, `exit`, `out`, `stop`, `bye`, and their non-English equivalents. Some remote systems will recognize that you telnetted into them. When you close the session properly, they will also close your telnet session. To close other connections, you may need to use a telnet convention for closing: `esc-comma`, `PA1`, or `control-]` and type `q` for quit.

When I telnet to my node, it usually works fine; sometimes I try and it doesn't work at all.

6.11

Again, circumstances come into play. Are the attempts always from the same place? At the same time of day? With the same equipment? Trying to find a variation in the pattern is key to understanding what's wrong, since the connection works sometimes. The failures may be because the system is very busy, shut down for maintenance, or because of incompatibilities. Even weather can be a factor! When you have gathered the pertinent facts, it may be useful to contact your local help desk.

6.12

I don't know how to find out where I can telnet to.

Some telnet programs, such as NCSA/BYU Telnet, actually carry a suggested host or two in their software menus. Special telnet clients provide access to particular telnet hosts; for example, Hytelnet supports connections to library catalogs and databases. Most systems available via telnet require a valid account for their use; many also allow certain limited services to be accessed either without login or via guest login. In addition to library catalogs, universities often allow remote access to their campus-wide information services (CWIS). Many printed Internet guides list popular sites for telnetting.

6.13

I have a telnet software package, but it won't open.

It sounds like you haven't installed the local TCP/IP driver, or you have installed it improperly. To use telnet, you need not only the telnet software but also the underlying software it needs to "speak" Internet.

Troubles with Telnet

Troubles
with FTP

7

FTP (file transfer protocol) is a key part of the TCP/IP proto-col suite. It allows you to move files from one place to another. FTP allows you to *get* files from and, under certain circum-stances, *put* files onto someone else's computer. Anonymous FTP allows you to sign on as a guest and get limited privileges to access files. As a result of FTP, many documents can be published quite easily over the 'net, encouraging a wide distri-bution of ideas. Beginning FTPers are often the most frustrated of all network users unless they are lucky enough to have access to some FTP software that translates FTP commands.

I want to FTP a file, but when I connect to the machine with the file I am challenged for an ID and password.

7.01

There are two kinds of FTP. The FTP protocol requires access privileges to the remote machine to *get* or *put* files. This means you will need a valid ID and password for the machine that has the file, or onto which you want to copy a file. Contact the owner of the server to get your account and password.

A special flavor of FTP is "anonymous FTP." Anonymous FTP allows users to connect as guests to *get* and *put* files; the protocol is to login to the remote machine with the userid: anonymous. You then use your complete electronic mail address as the password. That is the way that the remote machine keeps track of who connects to it.

For the most part, anonymous FTP only allows copying files onto your own machine (the *get* function). A few sys-tems allow anonymous copying of files to the machine (the *put* function), usually in a special directory—e.g., the incom-ing directory. Because a computer is especially vulnerable if anyone can write to its disk space, most FTP archives do not allow users to write to them. The large archives of shareware are an exception. In order to promote the deposit of programs by their authors, they will often allow the *put* function.

7.02 I tried to get a file and it didn't work.

Was your login successful? FTP archives are often very busy (see figure 7.1). Many of the largest have had to place restrictions on how many simultaneous connections they will sup-

```
220-
220-  Welcome to                              wuftpd 2.1c installed
220-  the U of M Software Archives                -- rjc@umich.edu
220-
220-  carpediem.ccs.itd.umich.edu is brought to you by
220-          U of M's Campus Computing Sites
220-
220-  Local Time:  Sun Mar 13 17:56:31 1994
220-
220 carpediem.ccs.itd.umich.edu FTP server (Version wu-2.1c(1) Thu Feb 3 22:20:50 EST
1994) ready.

530-
530-   All  allowed  connections  are  being  used  at  this  time.
530-
530-Due to overwhelming usage during business hours, restrictions to ftp access
530-are now being enforced.  PLEASE be considerate and ftp during non-"business
530-hours" as much as possible.  Also, please keep connection times short.
530-
530-Weekends:                                             60 connections
530-Weekdays from 11pm 'til 4am (EST):                    60 connections
530-Weekdays from 6pm 'til 11pm, and 4am 'til 6am (EST):  30 connections
530-Weekdays from 6am 'til 6pm (EST) ("business hours"):  10 connections
530-
530-The best way to access the archive files is via AFS.  If you have
530-AFS installed, "cd" or make a link to /afs/umich.edu/group/itd/archive.
530-
530-We also have three mirrors that are updated daily:
530-
530-          "wuarchive.wustl.edu" in the directory
530-                  /systems/{apple2,mac,atari,ibmpc,next}/umich.edu
530-     "src.doc.ic.ac.uk"     in the directory   "packages/mac/umich",
530-  and  "archie.au"          in the directory   "micros/mac/umich".
530-
530-Connecting to  mirror.archive.umich.edu  will automatically connect you
530-to one of the above mirrors.
530-
530 User  anonymous  access  denied.
```

FIGURE 7.1

Example of Fetch 2.1.1 FTP session to mac.archive.umich.edu denied because all sessions are in use. Note the restrictions on the numbers of sessions and the availability of mirrors, especially those in the United Kingdom (uk) and Australia (au).

port. No computer can handle an infinite number of connections at one time. It's possible that you didn't actually have a live session with the site. You might try to FTP during off-hours, not during the target site's prime business hours. Remember, over the 'net you can reach many international sites, so when it's daytime in the United States it may be the middle of the night halfway around the globe.

Could you see the file in the directory in which you are working? That's always the first thing to investigate. Enter the command `dir` to see where you are. Use the command `cd <directory or pathname>` until you can actually see the file. Be certain that you see the actual file and not a directory with the same name (see figure 7.2).

```
ftp is.internic.net
VM TCP/IP FTP V2R2
Connecting to IS.INTERNIC.NET 192.153.156.15, port 21
220-
220-|*******************************************************
220-|**                                                   **
220-|**   Welcome to the Internic InfoSource Archive      **
220-|**                                                   **
220-|*******************************************************
220-
220-
220-|General Atomics makes no warranty or guarantee, express or
220-|implied, concerning the content or accuracy of the information
220-|stored and maintained by General Atomics for the InterNIC Information
220-|Services and made available to INTERNET users, and General Atomics
220-|expressly disclaims any implied warranties of merchantability and
220-|fitness for a particular purpose.
220-
220-|For REGISTRATION Services,          please ftp to rs.internic.net
220-|For DIRECTORY AND DATABASE Services, please ftp to ds.internic.net
220-|For INFORMATION Services,           please login as user "anonymous"
220-                                     and cd /infosource
220-
220-
220-
220-|Questions? Send e-mail to info@internic.net
220-
220-
220 is FTP server (Version 2.0WU(10) Thu Apr 8 17:52:08 PDT 1993) ready.
USER (identify yourself to the host):
anonymous
>>>USER anonymous
331 Guest login ok, send your complete e-mail address as password.
Password:<userid@node>
```

Continued

FIGURE 7.2

This is the transcript of a VM/CMS FTP session to `is.internic.net`. The directory /pub is highlighted in the listing of the root directory, the `cd /pub` command changes to the pub directory, and then its contents are listed with the `dir` command.

```
>>>PASS ********
230-
230-Logged Access from: UICVM.UIC.EDU
230-
230-IMPORTANT NOTE:
230---------------
230-If you have problems accessing this archive:
230-Try using a dash (-) as the first character of your password
230-This will turn off the continuation messages that may
230-be confusing your ftp client.
230-
230 Guest login ok, access restrictions apply.
Command:
dir
>>>PORT 128,248,2,150,192,146
200 PORT command successful.
>>>LIST
150 Opening ASCII mode data connection for /bin/ls.
total 16
-rw-rw-r--    1 0        refdesk        237 Mar  8 08:32 .Links
drwxrwxr-x    3 0        1              512 May 27  1993 .bwaisindex
-rwxr-xr-x    1 0        0              293 Mar 13 22:58 .cache
-rwxr-xr-x    1 0        0              396 Jan 26 21:13 .cache.html
drwxrwxr-x    2 refdesk  refdesk        512 Jul 15  1993 .cap
drwxrwxr-x    4 refdesk  refdesk        512 Mar 27  1993 .ds
drwxrwxr-x    3 0        1              512 Mar  3 02:55 .waisindex
drwxr-xr-x    2 refdesk  refdesk       1024 Feb 25 08:15 .waisindex.old
drwxrwxr-x    4 refdesk  1              512 Mar  5 12:15 about-internic
dr-xr-xr-x    2 0        8              512 Mar 10  1993 bin
dr-xr-xr-x    2 0        8              512 Dec 17 03:34 dev
dr-xr-xr-x    3 0        8              512 Mar 10  1993 etc
drwxrwxr-x   12 refdesk  refdesk        512 Mar  2 19:11 infosource
dr-xr-xr-x    3 0        refdesk        512 Oct 21 21:31 pub
drwxr-xr-x    2 0        0              512 Feb 16 10:21 tmp
dr-xr-xr-x    3 0        3              512 Mar 10  1993 usr

Command:
cd /pub
>>>CWD /pub
250-Please read the file README
250-  it was last modified on Thu Apr  1 09:14:23 1993 - 346 days ago
250 CWD command successful.
Command:
dir
>>>PORT 128,248,2,150,192,155
200 PORT command successful.
>>>LIST
150 Opening ASCII mode data connection for /bin/ls.
total 2
-rw-rw-r--    1 0        1              110 Apr  1  1993 README
drwxrwxr-x    2 0        1              512 Aug 24  1993 jobs
226 Transfer  complete.
Command:
quit
>>>QUIT
221 Goodbye.
```

Did you type the name *exactly* as it appears, respecting capitalization and spacing? Be sure to check 1 and l and i, 0 and O.

Did you see the message: "transmission successfully completed"? If not, try again.

7.03

Someone says I can get something with FTP. She told me it was at `iitf.doc.gov` and referred to it as `pub/papers/documents/nii_agenda_for_action.txt`. What does that mean and how do I get there?

It means that you should open your FTP client and start a session at `iitf.doc.gov`. After you have logged on as `anonymous` with your `<userid>` as the password, you will need to navigate through the following directories: find the `pub` directory; in it should be a subdirectory called `papers`, which should in turn have another subdirectory called `documents`, in which the resource you want is located. You may do this in one step by entering the command `cd /pub/papers/documents` or in several steps by entering `cd /pub`, etc. When you have the subdirectory (`/pub/papers/documents`) active, you can `get nii_agenda_for_action.txt`.

Note: Citations for FTP files are notoriously inaccurate or incomplete. Usually a little adventurous sleuthing can locate the correct server address or path to the file.

7.04

I got a file, but I can't find it.

Did you tell the FTP server where to put the file when it got it and what to call it? Did you look around on your machine in case another directory or folder was the active one?

7.05

I got a file, but I can't read it.

What kind of file were you transferring?

Was it a text file? That's the default file transfer for FTP. Use the command `set ascii` to make certain that the file is being transferred as text.

Was it a program file? The default file transfer is ASCII text, so you will need to reset the mode for a program.

Use the command set binary to make certain that the program is being transferred correctly. You still may have to use a converter to get the program ready to run (see **8.05**).

Note: Macintosh BinHex program files should be transferred as ASCII text.

Did you get the message that the file had been transferred successfully? If not, you may need to try again. Watch the messages. Maybe you didn't have enough space to store the file. Maybe the file itself is corrupt.

7.06 I got something from an FTP server. Now what?

If it's an ASCII text file, you should be able to look at it using any word processor or text editor. If it's not ASCII text, then look at **8.05**, **8.06**, and **8.07**.

7.07 I connected to an FTP site and I could see the file, but the computer won't give it to me.

This usually means one of the following:

1. For some reason (probably beyond your control), the file isn't available. Try again later; repeat until successful.

2. You aren't typing the name of the file correctly or you have the wrong name (double-check the name in the directory).

3. You don't have enough room at your end to store the file (make some more space available before trying).

4. There's a network problem (try again later).

5. You aren't transferring the file correctly according to file type (see **7.05**).

6. You're trying to transfer a directory and not a file (check the directory to make certain that the name you see isn't the name of a subdirectory instead of the filename; sometimes files and directories have the same names).

7. The format of your command is wrong (check the instructions for your software or for the FTP protocol).

Troubles with FTP

My friend told me that a certain file was at a certain site. I went there, but I can't find the file.

7.08

Did you check all the directories off the main directory? The file may not be in the root directory but is instead in a subdirectory. Maybe your friends gave you the wrong site or the wrong <filename>. And, last but not least, the owner of the site may be updating the file so that it isn't available. Ownership of a server carries with it the responsibility to keep the server up all of the hours it is supposed to be available and to keep the files available at all times, but sometimes that just isn't possible.

I connected to the FTP source and I got the file, but I can't disconnect.

7.09

So many ways to conclude sessions on the Internet (see **1.05**); so little time and space! Fortunately the FTP protocol almost always supports the command: quit.

 There are some servers that won't close, no matter what. The only way out of these is to force a closing by terminating your communication software or hardware.

No matter what I do, I only seem to get about half the file.

7.10

There's the theoretical answer that only half the file is there, but that's not the likely explanation. More likely is one of the following:

1. You only have space for half the file (clear some space).

2. There's a bad character halfway through the file that keeps stopping the transfer (there should be an error message if this is the case).

3. You did get the whole file, but your machine doesn't have enough memory available to show you the entire file.

4. The method you are using to look at the file has some built-in restrictions on how much of the file you can view.

I'm tired of all these commands. Is there something easier?

There are several FTP clients out there. One of the most popular ones for the Macintosh is called Fetch (it's © Dartmouth College) and widely available on the 'net, including from Dartmouth's own FTP server at `ftp.dartmouth.edu`. For the DOS and Unix worlds, most telnet packages also support FTP, and there are archie (see **7.14**) clients to locate FTP sites; several DOS and Unix packages are now offering the graphical FTP approach as well.

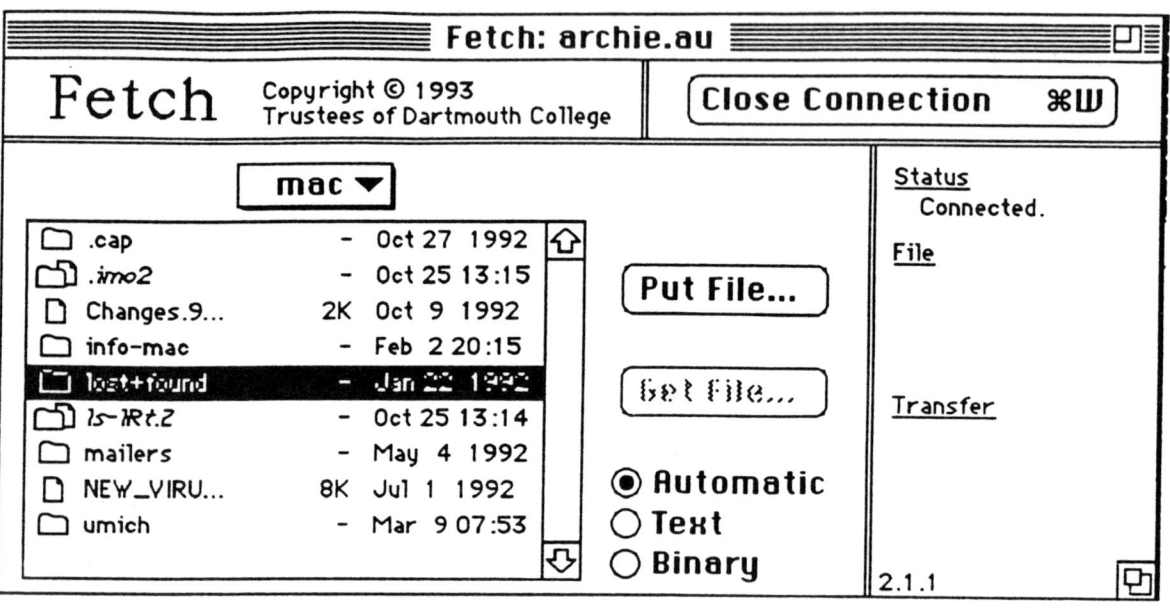

FIGURE 7.3
Window showing Fetch FTP session with `archie.au`'s FTP server in the micros/mac subdirectory.

Most second-generation clients (e.g., Internet Gopher and Mosaic) have FTP built into them so that a special client isn't needed. The remote FTP server must be available via an Internet Gopher server or Mosaic-compatible server.

I connected to the FTP server, but it wanted a login. What do I do?

If the server supports anonymous FTP, then login using the userid anonymous (if rejected, try the variations Anonymous and Guest or guest). The problem may be that the server doesn't support anonymous access. In that case, you need to get an ID and password from the owner of the server.

I want to put up some files to allow FTP to them. What do I do?

First, you need a computer, an Internet connection, and an operating system that'll handle both the computer and its connection. You'll need to get the software to manage the FTP server for your operating system. Then you need to structure your files and decide on the formats in which to make them available. Once that's done, just announce its availability on one of the network lists. If you build it, they will come!

 Lots of avid networkers copying files from your computer all day (and night) can crowd you out of your own machine.

Is there an index to FTP sites?

Yes, and since it's an index to FTP <u>arch</u>ives, it's called archie. Archie is available on the Internet via various Internet tools: <u>telnet</u>, <u>Internet Gopher</u>, <u>Mosaic</u>, and special archie clients. Archie is a keyword index to documents and sites reachable via FTP. The main archie server was quickly swamped with searchers, so now there are a number of servers available across the network. There are also a number of lists of FTP sites. One is maintained at the University of Illinois at Urbana-Champaign and is available via <u>Internet Gopher</u> at vixen.cso.uiuc.edu, under the menu item "Internet File Server (FTP) sites."

How can I connect to archie?

You can telnet to a special archie server and use its interface, you can use one of a variety of Internet gateways, or you can use your own archie client. Major archie servers are located around the world. Here is the list from the FTP FAQ (Frequently Asked Questions):

`archie.ans.net` (North America)

`archie.sura.net` (North America)

`archie.mcgill.ca` (Canada)

`archie.funet.fi` (Finland/Mainland Europe)

`archie.au` (Australia/New Zealand)

`archie.doc.ic.ac.uk` (Great Britain/Ireland)

`archie.unl.edu` (North America)

`cs.huji.ac.il` (Israel)

Is archie the same thing as <u>WAIS</u>?

Archie searches for strings of characters as they appear in menus and file or resource names. <u>WAIS</u> searches the complete text (once it's been properly indexed) for keywords.

Troubles
with Files

8

There are millions of computers, thousands of software packages, and hundreds of potential computer file types. Does it always seem that the file you want is unreadable on your machine? How can you avoid having a file look like hieroglyphics to you and your computer? Are there symbols or codes to help you avoid this heartbreak of digital junk on your display?

What are those characters at the end of the filename? Like .txt, .ps, and .hqx.

Files are identified by their name and an extension, to tell you what kind of file you're dealing with (see figure 8.1). A file labeled `stanhope.txt` means that the document is known as stanhope and that it is an ASCII text file. ASCII is the Esperanto of computers; any text saved as ASCII can be read by any computer and any word processor. Another common file extension is .doc for uncompressed text.

.ps means that a file is PostScript formatted so that any PostScript printer can publish it. PostScript is Adobe Systems' language that describes how files appear on paper and on your screen.

.hqx means that a file is stored in BinHex format, another universally readable format for FTP-able files.

Extensions are part of the description of DOS directories and files. You can't work with them unless you know the file's complete name, including its extension, if any. Macintosh users are saved from this burden, and can use as many as 31 characters to describe their files; extensions are completely optional.

```
ftp> cd /archie/clients
250-Please read the file README
250-  it was last modified on Wed Apr 15 10:00:00 1992 - 714 days ago
250 CWD command successful.
ftp> dir
200 PORT command successful.
150 Opening ASCII mode data connection for /bin/ls.
total 4651
-rw-r-----   1 root      daemon      42830 Jun 27  1993 MIRROR.LOG
-r--r--r--   1 15        ftp        305547 Mar  2  1992 NeXTArchie.tar.Z
-r--r--r--   1 15        ftp          1011 Apr 15  1992 README
lrwxrwxrwx   1 root      daemon         11 May 15  1992 archie-1.3.2.tar.Z -> kehoe.tar.Z
-r--r--r--   1 15        ftp        166623 May 21  1993 archie-1.4.1-FIX.tar.Z
-rw-r--r--   1 root      daemon     142802 Oct 25  1992 archie-1.4.tar.Z
-r--r--r--   1 15        ftp         73212 Feb  3  1992 archie-dos.zip
-r--r--r--   1 15        ftp          1199 Jan 13  1992 archie-one-liner.sh
lrwxrwxrwx   1 root      daemon         10 Jun  8  1992 archie-pc.nfs4.0.exe -> barber.exe
-r--r--r--   1 15        ftp        261881 Apr 29  1992 archie-vms.com
-r--r--r--   1 15        ftp        253480 Jan 15  1992 archie-vms.com.old
lrwxrwxrwx   1 root      daemon          8 May 28  1992 archie-vms.dcl.email -> atkinson
-r--r--r--   1 15        ftp          2334 Jan 13  1992 archie.el
-r--r--r--   1 15        ftp         73212 Feb  6  1992 archie.zip
-r--r--r--   1 15        ftp          6549 May 27  1992 atkinson
-r--r--r--   1 15        ftp        106249 Jun  8  1992 barber.exe
-r--r--r--   1 15        ftp         66797 Oct 11  1991 c-archie-1.1.tar.Z
-r--r--r--   1 15        ftp        222496 Nov 21  1991 c-archie-1.2-for-vms.com
-r--r--r--   1 15        ftp         98517 Nov 21  1991 c-archie-1.2.tar.Z
-r--r--r--   1 15        ftp        253480 Jan 13  1992 c-archie-1.3.1-vms.com
lrwxrwxrwx   1 root      daemon         11 Mar 15  1992 c-archie-1.3.1.tar.Z -> kehoe.tar.Z
-r--r--r--   1 15        ftp        261881 Apr 15  1992 c-archie-1.3.2-vms.com
-r--r--r--   1 15        ftp        115709 Apr 15  1992 c-archie-1.3.2.tar.Z
-r--r--r--   1 15        ftp        147328 Oct 28  1992 c-archie-1.4.1.tar.Z
-r--r--r--   1 15        ftp        142802 Oct 24  1992 c-archie-1.4.tar.Z
lrwxrwxrwx   1 root      daemon          9 Mar 15  1992 emacs-archie -> archie.el
-r--r--r--   1 15        ftp        179119 Nov 12  1991 ferguson.tar.Z
-r--r--r--   1 15        ftp        115709 Apr 29  1992 kehoe.tar.Z
-r--r--r--   1 15        ftp         27697 Aug 29  1991 khun.tar.Z
-r--r--r--   1 15        ftp         10381 Jan 13  1992 log_archie-pll.tar.Z
-r--r--r--   1 15        ftp         27697 Oct 11  1991 perl-archie-3.8.tar.Z
-r--r--r--   1 15        ftp        305547 Feb 19  1992 stark.tar.Z
-r--r--r--   1 15        ftp        192979 Oct 11  1991 xarchie-1.1.tar.Z
-r--r--r--   1 15        ftp        160842 Oct 11  1991 xarchie-1.2.tar.Z
-r--r--r--   1 15        ftp        179119 Dec 12  1991 xarchie-1.3.tar.Z
-r--r--r--   1 15        ftp        430567 Apr 26  1993 xarchie-2.0.1.tar.Z
-r--r--r--   1 15        ftp           274 Dec 12  1991 xarchie.README.NEW
-r--r--r--   1 15        ftp         54511 Oct 11  1991 xarchie.patch-1.2.shar
-r--r--r--   1 15        ftp         84699 Dec 12  1991 xarchie.patch-1.3.Z
226 Transfer complete.
2944 bytes received in 0.5 seconds (5.7 Kbytes/s)
ftp> quit
221 Goodbye.
```

FIGURE 8.1

List of files available via FTP from the directory /archie/clients at archie.au. Note the file names and the variety of file extensions.

Troubles with Files

**Do some file extensions refer to compressed files?
What is meant by "compression"?**

To save space on hard disks and make files less elephantine
as they travel over networks, compression utilities are used to
reduce the size of files. These programs use several methods
to shrink files, such as measuring frequent characters and
replacing them with a special code. To uncompress or restore
a file to its old self, you may need a copy of the utility that
originally reduced it. Some utilities can handle multiple
compression formats. File extensions identify the utilities
used in compression. For a table of basic compression-
decompression utilities, check the file `/doc/pcnet/com-`
`pression` at `stp.cso.uiuc.edu`.

.z and .Z are Unix compression utilities. To uncompress
files with the codes .z or .Z, type `unpack <filename>`
`.z` or `.Z` or `gunzip <filename>` `.z` or `.Z`.

.shar or .Shar, .tar, .TGZ, or .TAZ are other Unix compression forms.

.zoo exists both in Unix and DOS.

.zip is a DOS signal for the PKZIP utility, usually located
as `PKZnnn.exe`.

.gz is another DOS format akin to PKZIP; type `gunzip`
`<filename>` `.z` to uncompress a file.

.ARC, .LHZ, .ARJ, and .LHA are other DOS formats.

.Hqx or .hqx represents a Macintosh file needing a program known as BinHex.

.sit or .Sit identifies a Macintosh Stuffit file.

**I typed the name STANHOPE.DOC to pull a file
off another computer, and it didn't do a thing.
What's wrong?**

Some computers are sensitive creatures, specifically case-
sensitive. You may have been trying to read a file stored on a
Unix-based computer; Unix is a case-sensitive operating system. You need to ask for `stanhope.doc`, not `Stanhope.Doc`,

which might be another file altogether. To be completely Unix correct, you also should know that Unix files do not start with + or -. Unix filenames can contain letters, numbers, periods, -, _, or +. Unix filenames on some Unix systems have an upper limit of 14 characters; new Unix systems can deal with longer names. If you're a DOS user, remember that Unix directories are separated by / and not by your usual DOS \.

8.04 I'm stuck with tar. Am I going into the La Brea tar pits?

tar is a Unix abbreviation for "tape archiver." If you download a file labeled as tar, it means that the file consists of several parts which have been compressed together in one unit. You'll need to extract the files to make them usable on your computer. The Unix command `tar -tf <filename>` tells the computer to list contents. The Unix command `tar -xf <filename>` tells the computer to extract the files named after f. Remember that you need the proper utility to read `tar`.

```
ftp> cd /graphics/graphics/misc/figlet
250 CWD command successful.
ftp> dir
200 PORT command successful.
150 Opening ASCII mode data connection for /bin/ls.
total 48
-r--r--r--   1 graphics staff        5712 Aug  9  1993 figlet.readme
-r--r--r--   1 graphics staff       42198 Aug 10  1993 figlet.tar.Z
226 Transfer complete.
149 bytes received in 1.9 seconds (0.078 Kbytes/s)

ftp>
```

FIGURE 8.2
Example of directory with `tar.z` file that needs to be FTPed using the `bin` mode (see **7.05**).

8.05 I thought I downloaded a text file, but the output looks all crazy to me. Is this a binary file or an interplanetary transmission from Mars?

Files take two basic forms: as text, or ASCII, and as binary. Binary files are stored as binary values, zeros and ones. Why bother sending a binary file? Suppose you have an elaborately formatted bibliography saved in Microsoft Word. If you send

Troubles with Files

it as an ASCII file, all of your carefully contrived formatting is lost. You need to get the file across the continent today and can't afford to express ship a diskette. Well, you can ship the formatted file as binary and save all of your formatting.

The output will look like an interplanetary transmission, however, if your recipient does not have the proper utility to translate the binary file back into formatted Microsoft Word. In fact, your correspondent may need the same utility that you used to create the binary file in the first place. In Unix, the utility is uuencode, uudecode, and btoa (they also work for ordinary personal computers). BinHex is the utility for the Macintosh. Okay, so how does this work? To send your MS Word file, first take your utility, translate the Word document into binary, and then ship it as electronic mail. When your correspondent receives it, they use the same or, in some cases, another utility to reverse the process, carefully avoiding the headers of the electronic mail message in the process. Do your correspondent a favor by warning him or her where the binary file begins and where it ends, and describe the file's length in number of lines and characters. If it is an exceedingly long file, break it up into several parts.

Something is not right with a text file that I just downloaded. When I opened it in my word processor, the carriage returns and line endings looked weird.

8.06

Files created under different operating systems and different text processors will be formatted according to different conventions. You'll run into this problem especially when you're trying to view files on a DOS or Macintosh platform that were originally created under Unix.

Usually your file converter software can be set to correct for this sort of incompatibility. Check the instructions and manuals that are part of your converter utility package before you start to edit each line by hand. If you have no choice but to manipulate a document in order to make it readable, check out some of the features of your word processor (if it can open the file in the first place). Many word processors have Find and Change utilities that will help clean up erratic characters. A find-and-replace utility will help you get rid of bizarre characters in a document. To avoid the trouble of discovering how to reproduce the character on your keyboard, you can try to cut-and-paste the strange character into the utility.

I received a file that I thought was binary. I opened it after doing the utility magic with it, but it still looks intergalactic to me. What's wrong?

The file may be compressed. Some files are so large that the best way to ship them is to shrink them to a more convenient and cost-effective size. Compression utilities are identified by their file extension label at the end of a file name. .sit refers to a file compressed with a Macintosh utility known as Stuffit, .zip refers to PKZIP (DOS), .arc to ARC (DOS), and .Z to compress (Unix). In order to uncompress a file, you will need the utility that was used to compress it (see **8.02**) or a special decompressor.

I can only remember part of a filename on a remote computer. Is there a way to dig up all possible matches?

Many computers use symbols to stand for wild cards in order to help you search for files. In DOS, the asterisk (*) symbolizes one or several characters in a search. In Unix, there are several options. The question mark means that any character can be substituted at the location marked by the ?. So lea? may turn up leaf, leak, lean, or leap. An asterisk in Unix increases the possibilities for lea* to include learn, lease, leash, least, leather, leave, and leaven. Brackets in Unix like [ ] open the range of possible matches even further. These symbols can also be used with names for directories, if you're lost among a myriad of names and abbreviations.

```
ftp> mget *.doc
mget sqdate.doc? y
200 PORT command successful.
150 Opening ASCII mode data connection for sqdate.doc (10070 bytes).
226 Transfer complete.
local: sqdate.doc remote: sqdate.doc
10351 bytes received in 3.1 seconds (3.3 Kbytes/s)
```

FIGURE 8.3
Use of the * in the command mget *.doc locates the proper file sqdate.doc for transfer.

Can I move more than one file at a time?

8.09

First, you need to look at all of your file options and determine which files you'll need. If you're working in Unix, there are a few useful commands to know. *cd* changes the directory as in `cd /paleo/forams`; *ls* lists files in a specific location such as in `ls forams`. If you type `ls -1 forams`, you'll get additional information on file type and size. *mget* will move multiple files from a distant computer to your computer; *mput* will move multiple files from your computer to another machine. Prompts with *mget* will ask you if you want each file that falls into a specific search request. You can shut this prompt off by typing `prompt` before typing `mget`.

I looked at the contents of a directory in the long format with the *ls* command. What does all of that stuff mean?

8.10

Sure you want to know? See figure 8.4. The column labeled 1 tells you if you're looking at a file symbolized by a hyphen (-) or a directory noted by d. The columns beginning at the label 2 refer to the kinds of users who can deal with files and what they can do, such as x for execute, r for read, and w for write. There are three three-character groups that represent the owner, the group members, and, finally, others. The next column, labeled 3, tells you the number of files. The column labeled owner identifies the owner of the file. The last three columns give the file's size in bytes, when it was changed, and its name.

```
12              3 4        owner       size date time    name

-rw-rw-r--      1 0        refdesk     237 Mar  8 08:32 .Links
drwxrwxr-x      3 0        1           512 May 27  1993 .bwaisindex
-rwxr-xr-x      1 0        0           293 Mar 13 22:58 .cache
-rwxr-xr-x      1 0        0           396 Jan 26 21:13 .cache.html
```

FIGURE 8.4
Extract from the dir of an FTP session showing the results of an *ls* command.

I found a newsgroup with files of pictures. How do I download them?

You need to find and load the appropriate software to translate binary files to graphics on your computer. Binary files include characters outside the ASCII set. There are two utilities, uuencode and uudecode, that will help translate these files into something digestible for your computer. Uuencode translates binary to ASCII and uudecode translates it back. Often with larger files, it will be necessary to use uudecode to concatenate separate mail messages back into the original single file. This is not an easy process for beginners.

How would you recognize an ASCII form of binary? It would look quite like randomly collected characters, all strung together in a mail message. You might find a clue after the mail header, where the beginning of the file is noted with a message `begin`.... First of all, you'll need to download the binary file from your mail and save it for processing. Use uudecode to translate it to binary. It still may be compressed; watch for the telltale file extensions like .z after this conversion to provide a clue.

Troubles with Internet Gopher   9

Internet Gopher is almost too much fun to be troublesome. Almost. It's a relatively smooth ride, but watch out for tricky curves.

How do I get started with Internet Gopher?

9.01

Get yourself an Internet Gopher client. They are free and widely available for noncommercial use. The University of Minnesota makes many clients and servers (e.g., Turbo-Gopher for the Macintosh, PC Gopher and *DOS*gofer for DOS machines, and moog and xgopher for Unix) available via anonymous FTP at

        boombox.micro.umn.edu.

There are many other clients out there, so grab one and use it to explore.

Every time I want to use Gopher I can't get anywhere because the network is busy.

9.02

This is a real problem. Internet Gopher is one of the most heavily used Internet activities. Some Gopher servers are so popular that they can't handle all the traffic. The servers refuse attempts at connections when they are very busy. The answer to this problem is to try during off-hours.

Some Gopher servers allow connections only from certain domains because information available on the Gopher is licensed and its distribution must be restricted. The answer to this problem is to go somewhere else, to another Gopher.

Finally, you might hit a Gopher bottleneck in seeking a very popular menu, like Rice University's "The World by Subject" or Notre Dame's "The World by Phonebook." One way to circumvent the menus is to use Internet Gopher's "bookmark" feature to record the location of a favorite resource before you leave it. Next time, use the bookmark for a direct connection rather than tunneling through the menus. The really popular menus are duplicated widely. Go to another source rather than the originator of the menu.

9.03 I want to find a particular source on Gopher.

Just as <u>archie</u> is an index to <u>FTP,</u> veronica (Very Easy Rodent-Oriented Netwide Index to Computerized Archives) is an index to Internet Gopher. Regularly, the veronica programs read all of Gopherspace and make a keyword index to it. Veronica is available on a number of Internet Gopher menus. It is such a popular tool that a number of sites around the world now offer access to it because no single site could support all the users (see figure 9.1). Veronica supports searching of directory names only or searching of all titles. It has some fancy searching capabilities (a limited Boolean search) to assist in finding what you want out of the hundreds of thousands of Internet Gopher menu entries.

```
Rice CMS Gopher 2.4.2                              uicvm.cc.uic.edu
1/5
                  Veronica: Netwide Gopher Menu Search

<document>   How to Compose Veronica Queries
<search>     Search Gopher Directory Titles at NYSERNet
<search>     Search Gopher Directory Titles at PSINet
<search>     Search Gopherspace at PSINet
<menu>       Veronica at University of Nevada at Reno
```

FIGURE 9.1a
Veronica is accessible at several sites. In this search, we'll use veronica at NYSERNet in Syracuse, New York.

```
Rice CMS Gopher 2.4.2                        uicvm.cc.uic.edu
Enter keyword(s): dinosaurs

<document>  How to Compose Veronica Queries
<search>   Search Gopher Directory Titles at NYSERNet
<search>   Search Gopher Directory Titles at PSINet
<search>   Search Gopherspace at PSINet
<menu>     Veronica at University of Nevada at Reno
```

FIGURE 9.1b

We'll search Gopher sites for files referring to dinosaurs with NYSERNet's veronica.

```
Rice CMS Gopher 2.4.2                       empire.nysernet.org
1/27        More

    Search Gopher Directory Titles at NYSERNet
<menu>       Dinosaurs
<menu>       Dinosaurs (Reply)
<menu>       Dinosaurs (Reply).1
<menu>       Dinosaurs (Reply).2
<menu>       Dinosaurs (Reply).3
<menu>       Dinosaurs (Reply).4
<menu>       Dinosaurs, White House et al
<menu>       Dinosaurs, White House et al (Reply)
<menu>       Dinosaurs, White House et al (Reply).1
<menu>       Dinosaurs, Whitehouse, et al
<menu>       Dinosaurs
<menu>       Dinosaurs (Reply)
<menu>       Dinosaurs (Reply).1
<menu>       Dinosaurs (Reply).2
<menu>       Dinosaurs (Reply).3
<menu>       Dinosaurs (Reply).4
<menu>       Dinosaurs (Reply).5
<menu>       Dinosaurs (Reply).6
<menu>       Dinosaurs.1
```

FIGURE 9.1c

Veronica at empire.nysernet.org provides a list of dinosaur hits on Gopher.

Is veronica a <u>WAIS</u> for Gopher?

No, veronica searches character strings in menus and files and resource names. <u>WAIS</u> (Wide Area Information Servers) searches keywords indexed in full-text resources on networks.

I want to remember how to get back to someplace.

That's why Internet Gopher's bookmark feature was developed. It remembers where something is located. All Gopher clients offer the ability to save a direct tunnel to a resource in a bookmark (see figure 9.2). Unfortunately that doesn't guarantee that the item or the route to it won't change. Typically, the manager of a Gopher server puts up the files and the menus grow, change, and develop over time. As menus coalesce, merge, and diverge, the paths will change. But even so, bookmarks are very useful.

```
Rice CMS Gopher 2.4.2                                    marvel.loc.gov
GOPCLI041I  Bookmark  2  saved.
                   Library of Congress (LC MARVEL)
<menu>      About LC MARVEL
<menu>      Events, Facilities, Programs, and Services
<menu>      Research and Reference (Public Services)
<menu>      Libraries and Publishers (Technical Services)
<menu>      Copyright
<menu>      Library of Congress Online Systems
<menu>      Employee Information
<menu>      U.S. Congress
<menu>      Government Information
<menu>      Global Electronic Library (by Subject)
<menu>      Internet Resources
<menu>      What's New on LC MARVEL
<menu>      Search LC MARVEL Menus




1= Help       2= Open      3= Return    4= Print      5= Save/Rcv 6= Find
7= Backward   8= Forward   9= Bookmark 10= Booklist  11=          12= Quit
```

FIGURE 9.2a
Item being referenced is displayed.

Rice CMS Gopher 2.4.2
1/2
                        Ed Valauskas's **Bookmarks**
            Bookmark 1 deleted.
<menu>   **Library   of   Congress   (LC   MARVEL)**

1= Help   2= Open   3= Return   4= Print   5= Save/Rcv 6= Find
7= Backward   8= Forward   9= Delete   10= Refresh   11=   12= Quit

FIGURE 9.2b
The user's view of the bookmark.

```
 LASTING  GLOBALV  A1  V 80  Trunc=80 Size=16 Line=17 Col=1 Alt=0

===== MAILSEND"OUTLOG.FILENAME"9403
===== MAILSEND"OPTNAME.1"OUTLOG.FILENAME
===== MAILSEND"OPTNAME.0"1
===== $U25112 "MAILER"ALASRV
===== LDBASE   "SID.UICVM"LISTSERV
===== LDBASE    SNODE UICVM
===== GOPHER    "BOOKMARK.2"1Library  of  Congress  (LC  MARVEL)
marvel.loc.gov   70
===== GOPHER   "BOOKMARK.0"2
===== GOPHER   "BOOKMARK.1"i          Bookmark 1 deleted.
===== * * * End of File * * *



====>
                                              X E D I T   1 File
```

FIGURE 9.2c
The software's (VM/CMS Rice Gopher 2.4.2) view of a bookmark.

I just looked at something in Gopher and when I went back a few minutes later it was gone.

Perhaps the owner went to a meeting and turned off his or her machine. Or the network link is out for some reason (see figure 9.3). Or maybe the menu was restructured while you were gone. Or maybe the name was changed. Or maybe you forgot where you were. Because menus can and do carry entries for remote menus, you may think that you are getting something from one place, when in fact it came from another. All Gopher clients offer a way to see where something is actually located—it's called viewing the attribute information of a source. That view will tell you whether you actually have an item or whether you have a pointer to someone else's item.

```
Rice CMS Gopher 2.4.2                                   uicvm.cc.uic.edu
1/11
                                The World
<menu>       Other Illinois Gophers
<menu>       University of Minnesota
<menu>       CICnet Gopher
<menu>       Library of Congress (LC MARVEL)
<menu>       Netnews: Usenet, news services, etc (local access only)
<menu>       United States Government  gophers
<menu>       Veronica - Netwide Gopher Title Index
<menu>       Gopher Jewels
<menu>       The World By Subject (from Rice)
<menu>       The World by Location (from Minnesota)
<menu>       The World By Phonebook (from Notre Dame)
```

FIGURE 9.3a
Without a bookmark, we'll chase the Gopher at the U.S. Geological Survey, first looking under the heading United States Government gophers.

```
Rice CMS Gopher 2.4.2                          peg.cwis.uci.edu
91/115       More
                    United States Government gophers
<menu>       U.S. Bureau of the Census Gopher
<menu>       U.S. Dept Agriculture ARS GRIN National Genetic Resources
<menu>       U.S. Dept Agriculture Children Youth Family Education
<menu>       U.S. Dept Agriculture Economics and Statistics
<menu>       U.S. Dept Agriculture Extension Service
<menu>       U.S. Dept Agriculture National Agricultural Library Plant
<menu>       U.S. Dept Commerce  Information Infrastructure Task Force
<menu>       U.S. Dept Commerce Economic Conversion Information Exchange
<menu>       U.S. Dept Education
<menu>       U.S. Dept Energy
<menu>       U.S. Dept Energy  Environment, Safety & Health Gopher
<menu>       U.S. Dept Energy  Office of Nuclear Safety
<menu>       U.S. Environmental Protection Agency
<menu>       U.S. Environmental Protection Agency Futures Group
<menu>       U.S. Environmental Protection Agency Great Lakes National
<menu>          U.S. Geological  Survey  (USGS)
<menu>       U.S. Geological Survey Atlantic Marine Geology
<menu>       U.S. House of Representatives Gopher
<menu>       U.S. Military Academy Gopher
```

FIGURE 9.3b

After several screens in the menu United States Government gophers, we locate the U.S. Geological Survey.

```
Rice CMS Gopher 2.4.2                          info.er.usgs.gov
19/26
                    U.S. Geological Survey (USGS)
<menu>       Reference
<menu>       Regulations
<menu>       Search of GopherSpace - Veronica
<menu>       The UofI Weather Machine
type h       USGSHome.html
<menu>       WAIS Gateway
<document>   lynx_it
<menu>          special  collections
```

FIGURE 9.3c

In the U.S. Geological Survey menu, we locate an area for further investigation, special collections.

```
                           special collections
type -          -1
<menu>          webmaster <webmaster@info.er.usgs.gov>
<document>      Sorry, we don't allow off-site access to these
documents
```

FIGURE 9.3d

But `special collections` is inaccessible to further Gopher prying.

9.07

Someone says I can find something in Gopher. She told me it was in `gopher.uic.edu/library/`.... What does that mean and how do I get there?

It means that you should open your Gopher client and start a session at `gopher.uic.edu port 70`, the normal connection for all gophers (technically, a connectionless—i.e., no remote login—session for exchanging data via the Internet Gopher protocol at telnet port 70 on the host machine). After you have retrieved the uic.edu root Gopher menu, select the menu listing Library and repeat this for the rest of the names in the string until you find the resource (see figure 9.4).

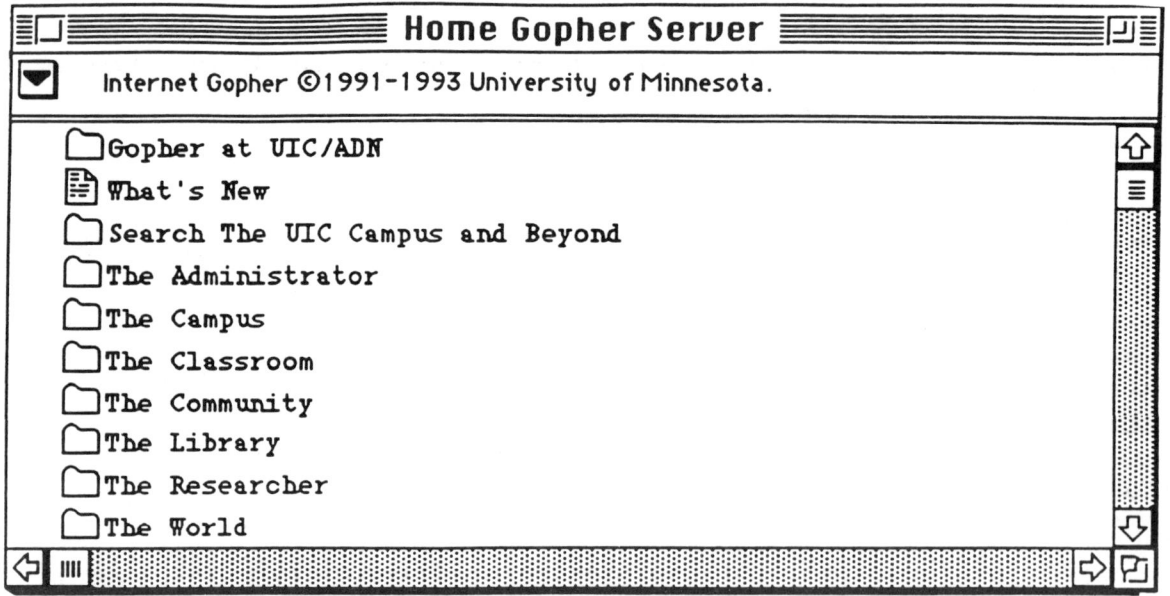

FIGURE 9.4

University of Minnesota's TurboGopher client for the Macintosh connected to `gopher.uic.edu port 70`.

I select something and the system says, "No files selected or available."

This probably means that the file isn't available. Why? There are a number of possibilities:

1. The menu has changed, and what you want doesn't exist under that name.

2. The file has been taken away.

3. The file is being updated or changed.

4. The client can't get through to the server.

The best strategy is to try again later. If you still don't succeed, then use veronica to find the current or another location for the item.

I saved a bookmark and tried to use it, but it didn't take me back to what it was supposed to.

That's the dynamic nature of Internet Gopher. Menu titles can and do change. So do document titles. Here today, gone or called something else tomorrow. Veronica can help find it; or if you know the hostname, use your client to connect to the root menu, and then look around to find where the item is now.

I asked for a file and the Gopher said it was getting it; but I can't find it.

Internet Gopher speaks FTP. Did you tell the Gopher client where to put the file when it got it and what to call it? Did you look around on your machine in case another directory or folder was the active one?

Troubles with WAIS, or Wide Area Information Servers 10

As you might have already discovered, the Internet hovers on the edge of chaos. How can anyone find anything? Chaos is the sort of "nontrivial" problem attractive to a breed of cybernauts, the type who invent, say, a new kind of super-computer. The engineers behind the Connection Machine, one of the first massively parallel supercomputers (transla-tion: it's very fast and very powerful), decided to tackle this problem of finding digital needles in electronic haystacks. First of all, they decided that computers talk best to other computers, not to humans. Computers can only talk well to other computers when they speak the same sort of language. Hence, special intercommunicating clients and servers were developed, among them the Wide Area Information Servers, or WAIS.

WAIS servers adhere to a standard language known as the WAIS protocol. WAIS is an extension of the National Information Standards Organization Z39.50 standard, which sets the parameters for remote information retrieval. With this protocol, WAIS designers were free to create an interface for humans.

WAIS clients allow users to search and retrieve docu-ments on WAIS servers using natural language keywords and search strings. WAIS servers and clients work together to report the relevance of items retrieved by rank, thanks to a built-in algorithm that weighs the search results. It seems so easy and librarian-like. So what can go wrong?

Is WAIS the <u>veronica</u> and <u>archie</u> of the Internet?

10.01

WAIS is much more (and much less) than <u>archie</u> and <u>veronica</u>. WAIS searches indexed full text by keywords. <u>Veronica</u> and <u>archie</u> only search characters in strings in <u>Gopher</u>, <u>FTP</u> directory, and resource name entries. WAIS will only search Internet resources for which a WAIS index has been created. Archie and veronica search for resources to point to and try to be as comprehensive as possible for their respective tools, FTP and Internet Gopher.

10.02 How do I get into WAIS if I don't have a WAIS client?

There are WAIS clients that can operate on your local computer, clients like HyperWAIS, which takes advantage of the Macintosh and HyperCard interfaces. There's WAIS software for Unix clients with an indexer and database server; you can get it by anonymous FTP think.com in the WAIS directory in a file labeled wais-8-b5.tar.z. You can find the Macintosh WAIS client at the same locale in the waistation-0-63.sit.hqx. HyperWAIS is available in the file /pub/freeware/mac/hyperwais.src.sea.hqx at ftp.wais.com. You'll also find WAIS for Windows, NeXT, OS/2, and IBM MVS. But to use your own client, you'll need to be connected directly into the network that communicates properly with WAIS servers.

If you don't have a WAIS client, you can connect to the WAIS home base by telnetting directly to quake.think.com and entering wais at the prompt for login. You'll be asked to identify yourself—provide your electronic address. When prompted for a terminal type, VT100 is always a safe bet (see figure 10.1).

```
Connecting to 192.31.181.1, port TELNET(23)


SunOS UNIX (quake.think.com)

login: wais
Last login: Sun Mar 13 12:42:33 from netcom4.netcom.c
SunOS Release 4.1.3 (SUN4C-STANDARD) #9: Wed Oct 27 18:18:30 EDT 1993
Welcome to swais.

Please type user identifier (optional, i.e user@host):
```

FIGURE 10.1
The initial prompt for WAIS at quake.think.com asks for your digital John Hancock (your electronic address).

This approach gives you a character-based terminal WAIS client. It's at the character level, so you'll miss all of the graphics on some clients. But now you have a chance to search (see figure 10.2).

```
This is the new experimental "wais" login on Quake.Think.COM

As the total number of sources has passed the 500 mark, we've found it's
become virtually impossible to find a source from the 25 screens of
sources.

I have decided that instead of presenting you with all the sources, I'll
just give you the Directory of Servers as a starting point.  To find
additional sources, just select the directory-of-server.src source, and ask
it a question.  If you know the name of the source you want, use it for the
keywords, and you should get that source as one of the results.  If you
don't know what source you want, then just ask a question that has
something to do with what you're looking for, and see what you get.

Once you have a list of results, you should "u"se the result you desire.
You can "v"iew a result before you "u"se it, paying close attention to the
"description".

Please let us know how you like this approach by sending feedback to
"wais@quake.think.com".

- WAIS at Think.COM

/notice.text
```

FIGURE 10.2
The welcome screen for WAIS at quake.think.com.

How can I be sure that I am reaching all the right servers?

Any experienced online searcher can tell you that the most important part of the search routine is done offline in preparation for a search. You can get a list of WAIS databases from quake.think.com by anonymous FTP. Think about your search in advance, and try to come up with a few keywords, just as you would prepare for a search on an expensive commercial database. Once you have a list of well-defined and unique keywords, and also an idea of what kinds of files you might need to look into, then access WAIS's metaserver, the Directory of Servers. The Directory of Servers will point you

Troubles with WAIS, or Wide Area Information Servers

to the appropriate WAIS servers to handle your query, also known as the

```
directory-of-server.src@quake.think.com.
```

There are more than 500 WAIS servers ready to help. Using the WAIS terminal client, once you're in the Directory of Servers, you hit the w-key to enter your keywords. Don't muddle your search with articles like "the," "and," or "an." WAIS will provide you with a list of servers that might have more information on your topic. Then you run your actual search against all or some of those servers to get the actual data.

10.04

There are so many servers on my topic! Can I preview them before I begin my search?

Again, in the WAIS terminal client, by hitting the space bar you can find out more information about each server before you approach it with a specific search. When you're ready to search, remember to deactivate the Directory of Servers from your list of searchable servers. You can do that by hitting the space bar. With WAIS clients for specific machines, these techniques will vary. You may have to double-click with a mouse, or type a command to achieve the same effect.

10.05

I'm getting a lot of junk in my search. How can I improve the results?

Veteran searchers will remind you of the old axiom "garbage in, garbage out" for online searching. Look at your search terms and think about whether they might be confusing to someone who doesn't understand their context. Could a term have several meanings? WAIS cannot decipher the meaning of a term or set of terms as well as you can.

Look at relevance scores for each of your hits in a server. The higher the score, the better WAIS has judged the information to match your own desires. A relevance score of 1,000 is perfect. You can refine the search further with WAIS's *similar to* search. With this function, you can mark entries found on the first search for further analysis by WAIS. WAIS then examines these entries and examines its servers again, looking for documents more like the chosen item. This sort of refinement makes WAIS a powerful search-and-retrieval engine.

Troubles with WAIS, or Wide Area Information Servers

I'm getting nothing in my search. The Directory of Servers says there's nothing about "trilobites" in any WAIS servers. What can I do?

The Directory of Servers is a general pointer to information contained in WAIS servers. There's a real danger of being specific, and finding nothing just because you used a term that was far too specific for this level of searching. Trilobites have nothing to do with kilobytes. They're extinct arthropods. Try backing up a level or two in your selection of terms. Try fossils or paleontology or geology, terms that might fit in at a more general sphere. Never take the WAIS answer of "No databases available" as an absolute No.

I'm confused about the kinds of commands that work in WAIS. Where can I find more information about them?

The WAIS interface that you're working in (if you aren't working with a specific client) is Unix-based. If you're not a Unix weenie, there's an easy way to get a short list of commands. Just type ? at the prompt and hit enter to get the basic list. If you're really into the technical details of the WAIS Interface Protocol, they are available by anonymous FTP at quake.think.com as /pub/wais/doc/protospec.txt. To understand that file description, see **7.03**.

How do Boolean searches work in WAIS?

Mathematician George Boole never thought his name would be used in vain like this. In 1854, Boole thought that any problem could be broken down with his logical operators. WAIS was designed for natural language queries. Boolean operators work in WAIS, but try searching without them. Compare your results to queries constructed with simple Boolean operators.

Can I WAIS from Gopher?

Yes, you can take advantage of WAIS from Gopherspace, even though the two systems take entirely different approaches to Internet resources. Most Gophers can get you to WAIS's Directory of Servers as a starting point, for example, by pointing to gopher.brown.edu. Once you've located servers of use to you, you can search them from within <u>Gopher</u> rather than changing to the WAIS client interface.

10.10

Can I eliminate some of the items in a search without using the *similar to* feature?

In WAIS, you can't refine searches on the fly as you're working your way through results. You also can't ask WAIS to tell you if a server's files have been updated recently, or restrict searches to only recent or new materials in servers. WAIS's relevance feedback in the *similar to* feature is the only way to distill searches online, and it is a most impressive tool. WAIS bases its retrieval by finding documents whose WAIS profile matches that of the document you have selected.

10.11

Could I use WAIS to index some files I have? I really would like to see something about trilobites out there.

You can construct a WAIS index for almost any file. Look for "waisindex" with WAIS or with <u>archie</u>. You can also secure it by anonymous <u>FTP</u> from think.com under the directory wais.

Troubles with WAIS, or Wide Area Information Servers

Troubles with World Wide Web

11

Near Geneva at the foothills of the Alps, scientists at the European Organization for Nuclear Research (CERN) study the interactions of subatomic particles, explore condensed matter and quarkonia, and think about The Standard Model. Ideas at CERN have generated a lot of information, terabytes of it (a terabyte is 1,099,511,627,776 bytes). Unfortunately, over time, much of this information was becoming more and more difficult to locate. Details of experiments—recording millions of interactions of particles—were effectively being buried in paper or computer files, not to be seen without an arduous search. To solve this problem and make scientific results more accessible, World Wide Web (WWW, or W^3) was invented. WWW links documents using hypertext.

Hypertext, Ted Nelson's almost science fiction notion of sewing together all intellectual output in one way or another by computers, in WWW really works. The Web connects text between documents by a series of imbedded links. These links are hypertext (see figure 11.1) and are identifiable by virtue of being highlighted or underlined. You simply click on a link and are taken away to the other end of the connection, which could be in the same document or in another file altogether. This hypertext adds value to documents by allowing each document to carry more content, by placing it in a sphere of reference with other materials. No document or file is an island in WWW.

Physical location is not an issue, as documents can be displayed and retrieved anywhere, no matter if a WWW server is around the corner or on another continent. World Wide Web encourages curiosity and allows for serendipity. There's more to WWW than just neutrinos or W bosons or superconducting magnets or antiprotons. A new WWW server appears about every day. There are hundreds of servers around the world covering a wide range of subjects.

THE WORLD-WIDE WEB

```
This is just one of many access points to the web, the universe of
information available over networks. To follow references, just type the
number then hit the return (enter) key.

The features you have by connecting to this telnet server are very primitive
compared to the features you have when you run a W3 "client" program on your
own computer. If you possibly can, please pick up a client for your platform
to reduce the load on this service and  experience the web in its full
splendor.

For more information, select by number:

A list of available W3 client programs[1]
Everything about the W3 project[2]
Places to start exploring[3]
The First International WWW Conference[4]

This telnet service is provided by the WWW team at the European Particle
Physics Laboratory known as CERN[5]
   [End]


1-5, Up, Quit, or Help:
```

FIGURE 11.1
The numbers in [ ] above indicate hypertext links to other documents.

WWW's connections to other Internet tools make using them a breeze. Just explore!

With WWW, you connect to a WWW server and use the server's interface to search for materials. Alternatively, you use a browser client created specifically for your computer, taking advantage of its own interface. The most archaic WWW browser works in old-fashioned line mode, but it *will* work with almost any computer or terminal. Line mode means that WWW options are identified by numbers. Type a number and hit <return> to select a specific option. WWW's browsing capabilities have been enhanced with a tool called Mosaic, if you're ready for a real Flash Gordon Internet tool. Mosaic takes advantage of WWW's hypertext capabilities and allows a networker to use his or her own machine as the client to a Web server. (For more information, see chapter 12.)

Troubles with World Wide Web

Where do I get a World Wide Web client?

You can reach CERN by telnetting to `info.cern.ch` or any of several WWW servers, then downloading a WWW browser specifically designed for your computer. The opening "front page" of World Wide Web tells you in line mode where to find client programs, where to start searching, or how to find more information about WWW.

Alternatively, there's a new tool called Lynx, a character-based intermediary to WWW. You can find it by anonymous FTP to `ftp2.cc.ukans.edu` in the `pub/lynx` directory. You can try out Lynx by telnetting to

`ukanaix.cc.ukans.edu` and logging on as `www;` or

`www.twi.tudelft.nl` and logging on as `lynx;` or

`millbrook.lib.rmit.edu.au` and logging on as `lynx.`

How do I get started?

Connect to CERN by telnetting to `info.cern.ch`, login, and operate in line mode. Suppose you decide to start searching in WWW by selecting option number 3, "Places to Start Exploring" (see figure 11.1).

This option takes you to a screen providing access to the World Wide Web by Subject, by Servers, and by Service Type (WAIS, Gopher, telnet, anonymous FTP, and so on) where you can search by subject or by type, or just learn more about WWW. Using World Wide Web is just that simple. Select an option identified by a number, use `<return>`, type `Help` for assistance, and type `quit` to leave WWW altogether. World Wide Web makes WAIS, Gopher, telnet, anonymous FTP, and other resources available without requiring an extraordinary knowledge of high-energy physics or computers on your part. It's a rocket science Internet tool for technopeasants.

I opened a document in World Wide Web and I can't move around in it. What do I need to do?

There's a basic suite of WWW commands that should be the linguistic models for all computer orders. These commands are simply: `Back` takes you to the last document you've reviewed; `BOttom` to the end of a document; `HOme` to the first document in a sequence; `List` for a reference list from a document; `Next` to the next hypertext connection in a document;

`Recall` provides a list of documents that you've examined; `Top` puts you on the first page of a document; and `Up` moves up a page in a document. If all is lost, type `Help` for WWW assistance online.

11.04 I'm lost! I need to get back to a document I looked at four files ago. How can I go back?

You can always go home in World Wide Web, or at least find your way around. WWW leaves a trail of cyber–bread crumbs, which you can invoke by using the *recall* command. A screen will appear, giving you a list of places that you've visited with WWW (see figure 11.2).

```
  Documents you have visited:-

R   1)    in Welcome to the World-Wide Web
R   2)    in Overview of the Web
R   3)    in The World-Wide Web Virtual Library: Subject Catalogue
R   4)    in Data sources classified by access protocol
R   5)    in The World-Wide Web Virtual Library: Subject Catalogue
R   6)    in United States Geological Survey-HTTP Server-Home Page
R   7)    in What's New With the U.S. Geological Survey
R   8)    in What's New With the U.S. Geological Survey
R   9)    President Names Eaton to Head USGS
R  10)    in Welcome to the World-Wide Web
```

FIGURE 11.2
Recall acts as your never-failing memory in World Wide Web to help you retrace your steps in cyberspace.

Each item in this list is numbered. Type `recall` followed by the number of the document that you would like to go back to. World Wide Web returns you just that simply.

11.05 I tried to get into <u>archie</u> via the World Wide Web, and it told me that it couldn't do that. Why?

WWW at CERN told you that <u>archie</u> access was "Forbidden" and "Unable to access." Like any network resource, WWW provides access to some resources locally and some remotely. The set of resources provided in Geneva is richer than those made available over the network. World Wide Web can provide you with clues to track down information with other tools on your computer such as <u>telnet</u> and anonymous <u>FTP</u>. For security reasons, public access will probably always mean that some features, in spite of being in plain view to you on the screen, do not operate.

But can I <u>FTP</u> with WWW?

11.06

Files are accessible by anonymous <u>FTP</u>, but World Wide Web alerts you with an understatement that it is a "nontrivial problem" (ah, the ever subtle wit of high-energy physicists) (see figure 11.3).

```
                              A to E: Exhaustive List of FTP Sites (23/998)

                 A TO E: EXHAUSTIVE LIST OF FTP SITES


a.cs.uiuc.edu 1                        128.174.252.1   US -5     90/08/22
Admin: Univ. of Illinois - Urbana-Champaign
Files: TeX; dvi2ps; gif; texx2.7; amiga; GNUmake; GNU

a.psc.edu 2                            128.182.66.105  US -5     90/12/31
Admin: Pittsburgh Supercomputing Center
Files: GPLOT; GTEX

aarnet.edu.au 3                        139.130.204.4   AU +10    92/12/20
Admin: Australian Academic & Research Network
Files: Australian AARNET network stats

acacia.maths.uwa.oz.au 4               130.95.16.2     AU +8     92/12/20
Admin: Univ. of Western Australia

acfcluster.nyu.edu 5                   128.122.128.11  US -5     91/01/02
Admin: New York Univ.
Server: 128.122.128.17, 128.122.128.16
Files: VMS UUCP; news; DECUS library catalog; vsmnet.sources; info-vax code
1-228, Back, Up, <RETURN> for more, Quit, or Help:
```

FIGURE 11.3
WWW provides a means to anonymous <u>FTP</u> with catalogs of sites.

Why? Files exist in a wide variety of types. Some are text files, but others are sound or graphics files, or a mixture of several types. You should never have a problem examining an uncompressed ASCII text. But how can you recognize problems in advance? Files exist with abbreviations at the end of their names, like .hqx, .tar, .Z, .sit, .ps, .gif, and so on (see **8.01, 8.02,** and **8.04**). Computers have problems with file types, too. Sometimes, it's easy for the computer to recognize a PostScript file as PostScript and identify it with the code .ps. But sometimes it's impossible for the computer to recognize a file, so it guesses at the file type. These guesses may make it difficult for you and your computer to deal with a downloaded file.

In addition, files can be compressed to conserve disk space on servers and make them less elephantine over the network. Without the correct decompression programs on your computer, it could be quite a problem to read certain files (see **8.02** and **8.04**). You can save yourself a lot of work by using a little common sense. If a file appears to be clearly identified as a binary file, then make sure your computer and telecommunications software transfer it as binary and not as text (see **8.05** and **8.07**). It will save you a lot of frustration. If a file is compressed, make sure you have the right decompression engine to make the file usable (see **8.07**).

11.07

Wait a minute. I thought I could look at images and listen to audio with WWW. What's going on?

You need a specific browser client and some special software to take advantage of all of the information on the World Wide Web. For example, if you visit the U.S. Geological Survey WWW server, the first prompt invites you to "look here 1." With the proper graphically based browser, you can view on your computer Vernal Falls in Yosemite National Park. In line mode, without the correct browser, all you'll see is text. Browsers, such as MacWWW on the Macintosh, the cello browser for MS Windows, or the *Viola* browser for XWindows, allow you to see (and even listen to) many files that just aren't available in line mode.

WARNING To make graphics and sound appear on your desktop with WWW and a suitable client, your computer needs to be directly wired to the network. It won't work if you're connected via a modem unless you use SLIP (Serial Line Internet Protocol) or PPP (Point-to-Point Protocol) to create an Internet connection over the telephone cable. Even so, many large files can be slow to move and expensive to transmit unless you have a direct connection.

You might not be able to look at audio or graphics files because you lack the proper playback equipment, so to speak, in your computer. You might not have sufficient RAM

Troubles with World Wide Web

to deal with the files, you may be missing the appropriate graphics card or software to display an image, or your motherboard might be missing a digital signal processor to properly play an exotic audio file. It may have nothing to do with WWW or your telecommunications package; to be blunt, your equipment might not be able to deal with the complexities of sophisticated files.

There's lots of stuff out in the wide WWW world. Are there any navigational tools like <u>archie</u> or <u>veronica</u> for WWW?

11.08

Unfortunately, not at this writing. One way of systematically attacking WWW is by its own subject catalog. Entries in this part of the WWW universe change rapidly, so if you don't find something today, check tomorrow or next week. Once you find yourself in a useful file, you might find on WWW's command line a prompt for `find` urging you to search on a keyword. These queries are made possible by <u>WAIS</u>.

Another way of approaching this hypertext universe is searching WWW services by type. You can find this option on the WWW home page. Once inside this listing, WWW will simply take you to any server by your merely selecting it. Some servers may not be completely operational, but you can't beat this option as a way to tour the world from your chair.

I have a creative idea about WWW. How can I contact one of the members of the WWW team?

11.09

You can use WWW to find out more about its creators. At the end of the options under By Service Type, there is a last obscure reference labeled "Tim BL : 28." Choosing this option will take you to a note by Tim Berners-Lee, the father of World Wide Web at CERN, and a means to learn more about him and the widely dispersed WWW team (including their electronic addresses). As you might expect, this is not the only path in WWW to this information.

11.10

**I tried to print but nothing happened.
What's wrong?**

Certain commands in World Wide Web work only for Unix-based computers. If there's a way your computer can save screens or download files, you should be able to print from them.

11.11

All of my text in World Wide Web appears with headings like SGML, HTML, New anchor, Linking anchor, and other strangeness. What's going on?

You're looking at the World Wide Web in verbose mode. It's a complete transcript of the Web reading information and passing it along from one computer to another. Type `Help` at the WWW command line and type `verbose` to toggle to non-verbose mode.

11.12

Do I always have to start from World Wide Web's front page when I start up?

You can customize WWW to start with a page of your own design or a front page located on another server. You need to set the variable WWW_HOME to the correct address of the page you'd like to use.

11.13

World Wide Web would seem like a great medium for a journal or magazine. Has anyone tried to format a periodical in it?

The venerable electronic edition of *Postmodern Culture* is now available in WWW, along with all back issues. FTP to `ftp.ncsu.edu` or Gopher to `jefferson.village.virginia.edu`. *Postmodern Culture* is also available on Macintosh diskette and microfiche from Oxford University Press.

Troubles
with Mosaic *12*

Mosaic should be called an advanced Internet tool because it is able to "speak" the basic protocols (<u>FTP</u> and <u>telnet</u>) as well as the second-generation protocols (<u>Internet</u> <u>Gopher</u>, <u>WAIS</u>, <u>World</u> <u>Wide</u> <u>Web</u>). What is Mosaic? It's a client that runs in the Macintosh, Windows, and Unix environments. Mosaic has been developed at the University of Illinois National Center for Supercomputing Applications (NCSA). It treats the Internet as a "mosaic" of services and systems and gives the networker a consistent graphic window for viewing and talking to it. It gives different systems a common feel, keeps track of where you are going and where you have been, and enriches the two-dimensionality of print with pictures and sounds. It has caught on quickly as the network's first generally usable and accessible client for talking the language of <u>World</u> <u>Wide</u> <u>Web</u> servers (see chapter 11).

If you don't have Mosaic, here's a start. You need to anonymous <u>FTP</u> a version of Mosaic from `ftp.ncsa.uiuc.edu`, unpack it, and load it onto your local system. Clients are available for Sun, DEC, MS Windows, RS/6000, and Macintosh computers. You have to be connected directly to the Internet to connect to a <u>World</u> <u>Wide</u> <u>Web</u> server. Mosaic comes configured to connect to NCSA's server. Business has gotten so brisk that the Center asks networkers to connect to the special Mac, Windows, and Unix front pages to reduce the amount of traffic on the original common home page (see figure 12.1). This trifurcation has allowed NCSA to point out some special features, e.g., things that the Mac client does and the Windows one doesn't, or vice versa.

Why is Mosaic so popular? After you listen to the Geek of the Week radio show, look at satellite weather photos, and see a jet engine propulsion animation, we may not have to answer this question.

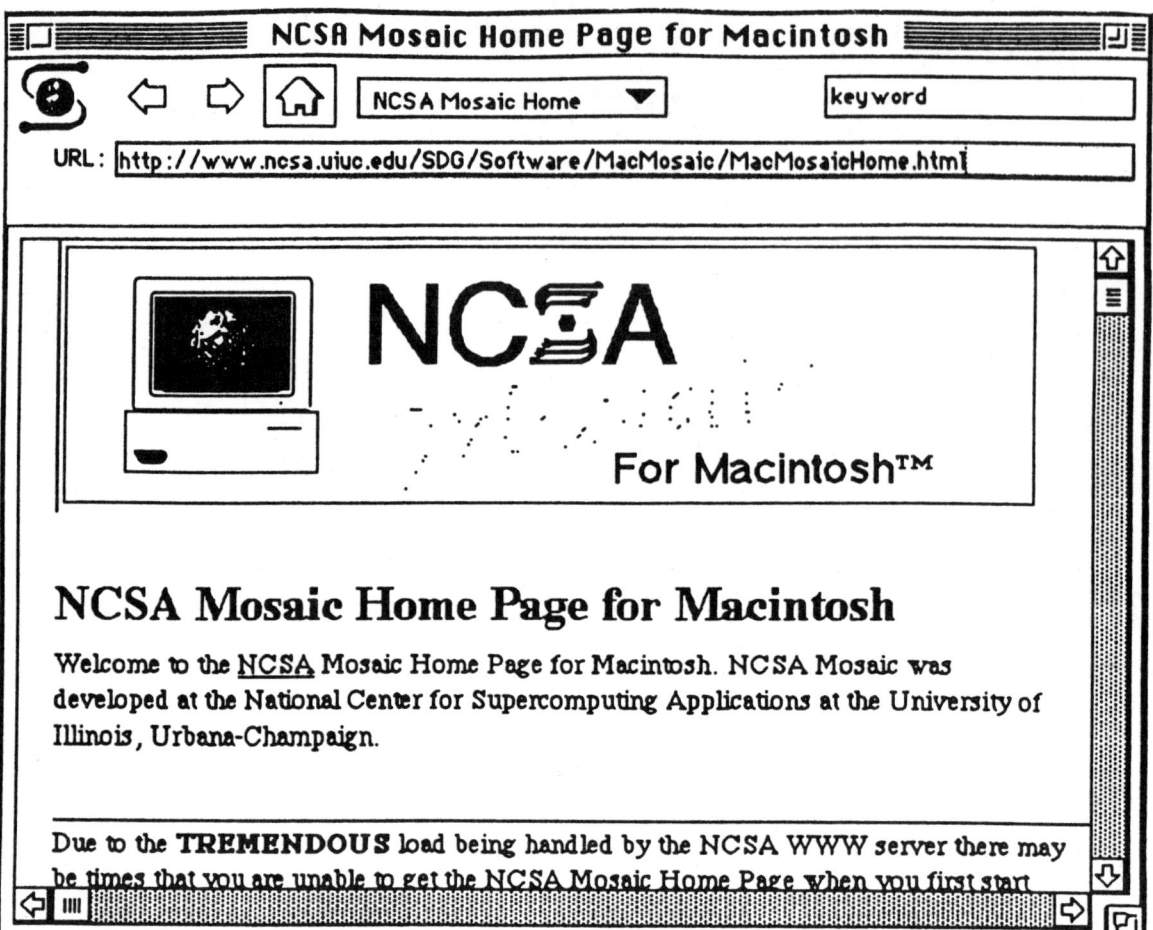

FIGURE 12.1

The Mosaic home page for the Macintosh advises the user that there may be problems connecting to the World Wide Web server at the University of Illinois National Center for Supercomputing Applications.

12.01

I tried to get a file, and it didn't work.

Mosaic will try to bring over the file and display it for you. Large files and files whose display will take more room than you have memory are stored on your hard drive, with a warning. Also, Mosaic will write files onto your drive as space allows to speed up your reference to these when you go back and forth in the menu of services visited. If you are not careful, Mosaic will eat up all your available space with its Temp files and with the files you actually tell it to store.

Also, each time you ask for the file, another copy of it will be brought over. It's quite easy to end up with several copies of a file. So look around carefully for any new files on your drive before you decide you didn't get the file.

I got a file, but I can't find it.

12.02

Look around; it's probably there. It may not have the name you expect, or be in the place you expect. Be creative.

I got a file, but I can't read it.

12.03

This is a common problem. Because Mosaic is a window to such a rich and diverse environment, it's easy to find files in formats your machine can't handle. For example, you won't retrieve just text, PostScript, and program files, but you'll also retrieve materials in graphic, audio, and video formats. You will need readers that can handle many different graphic formats, known as pict, tiff, jpeg, and gif. In addition to proprietary software that you can license from a software dealer, there are shareware and freeware readers for these files. Many readers are available from the Mosaic server at NCSA. You'll need a lot of readers and you'll still pull over some picture you can't read without stocking in another one.

Finally, you may have pulled over a file requiring special software or equipment you don't have available. Because Mosaic can access so many Internet sources so easily, accept the tradeoff of one you can't use.

I connected to the Internet with Mosaic and I could see a file, but the computer wouldn't give it to me.

12.04

Mosaic will show you a lot of great stuff. Just because you can see it on a menu doesn't mean that you'll be able to connect to it. Some of it can only be seen by certain users because it is specially licensed for their use; some of it may be too large or have some requirement that your equipment and software can't handle. The file may be a sound and your machine may be playing it, but your volume may not be turned up. Many resources have a README file. It may be boring, but reading README can answer a lot of questions.

12.05

My friend told me that an interesting file was at a certain site. I went there, but I can't find the file.

Files on the Internet are ephemeral. Their names change. The menus under which they appear often restructure. The servers on which they are located are turned off or their names change. Your software may be set only to show you files you can manage, so you may not see one on the menu if it is too large or in an inappropriate format.

12.06

I connected to a source and I got the file, but I couldn't disconnect.

Quitting a service can be as big a problem as finding it. Usually, though, you are told how to quit as you connect, or in the README file. So, don't press that clear key too fast. Read the instructions on the way in (take notes), and that will save you troubles on the way out. There are ways to exit gracefully (see **1.05**); the ungraceful exits are to hang up the phone line, close the client, or shut off your equipment!

12.07

No matter what I do, I seem to get only about half the file.

It sounds like you don't have enough space available for the file. Maybe you got all the file, but are unable to view it because of memory or software limitations. It's also possible that only half the file is available. Something may be wrong with the file so that the transfer fails halfway through. For example, some "garbage" character strings in the file may have the right sequence to tell the software to stop downloading. If you are using a phone line, troubles can be caused by noise on the line. And finally, you may have exceeded some preset limit on transferring files in or out of a site.

12.08

I found a radio broadcast and I brought it over, but when I try to play it nothing happens.

The first thing to check is whether the volume is turned up on your computer. Next, check the volume control in the software you are using to play the broadcast. If the volume settings are okay, then check to see if the entire file has been transferred, if the software is the right kind to play the file you located, and then if the software is up and running. If all that seems okay, then make sure that you have unzipped, unstuffed, decoded, or unpacked the file.

I know the address of a source, but I get an error message when I try to go to it.

12.09

Recheck the name of the site address. Upper- and lowercase is significant.

I forgot a friend's birthday. Someone told me that I can use a florist's shop via Mosaic. That's not possible, is it?

12.10

Grant's FTD Flowers are available via http with Mosaic. Http is the Hypertext transfer protocol used by WWW. To examine and select flowers on the Internet, start up Mosaic and just load the URL (Universal Resource Locator):

        http://florist.com:1080.

WARNING Send your credit card number over the Internet at your own risk.

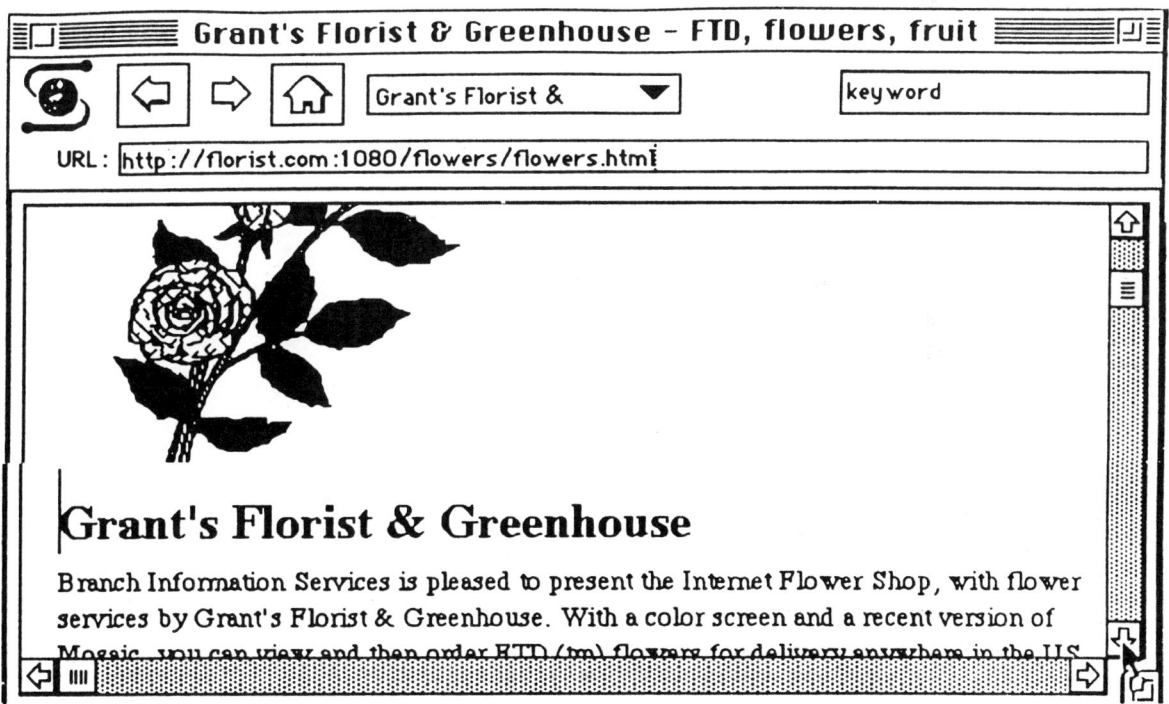

FIGURE 12.2
Shopping the electronic way with Macintosh Mosaic 1.0.3.

A Troubles Resource List *13*

Print

For paper devotees, there are tons of print materials about the Internet, the newest darling of the publishing industry. Some of these books are mere compilations of electronic resources on the 'net; others are classics, perfect Baedekers to this digital environment. This list does not pretend to be comprehensive; new titles appear on an almost daily basis. There seems to be no shortage of paper for a paperless modern world.

Dictionaries and Directories

If you're confused by computer terminology, or you've just been attacked online by a wave of acronyms, these dictionaries can help. You might find some of these highly entertaining reading in their own right.

Frey, Donnalyn, and Rick Adams
!%@:: A Directory of Electronic Mail Addressing and Networks
Sebastopol, Calif.: O'Reilly & Associates, 1990.
420 p., paper. ISBN 0-937-17515-3.

Godin, Seth
The Smiley Dictionary: Cool Things to Do with Your Keyboard
Berkeley, Calif.: Peachpit Pr., 1993.
73 p., paper. ISBN 1-566-09008-3.

Machovec, George S.
Telecommunications, Networking and Internet Glossary
Chicago: Library and Information Technology Assn., 1993.
124 p., paper. ISBN 0-838-97697-2.

Okerson, Ann (ed.)
*Directory of Electronic Journals, Newsletters and Academic
    Discussion Lists*
Washington, D.C.: Assn. of Research Libraries, 1993.
3d ed., 355 p., paper. ISSN 1057-1337.

Raymond, Eric S. (comp.)
The New Hacker's Dictionary
Cambridge, Mass.: MIT Pr., 1993.
2d ed., 505 p., paper. ISBN 0-262-68079-3.

Williams, Robin, and Steve Cummings
Jargon: An Informal Dictionary of Computer Terms
Berkeley, Calif.: Peachpit Pr., 1993.
676 p., paper. ISBN 0-938-15184-3.

Internet Guides for Beginners

A little knowledge is a dangerous thing, according to T. H.
Huxley. Huxley must have been dreaming about the Internet,
where his axiom is proved every day. These books can help
you correct misunderstandings and dismiss any fear about
electronic resources. Huxley also pointed out that irrationally
held truths may be more harmful than reasoned errors, cer-
tainly a description of the content of some messages on discussion lists.

Badgett, Tom, and Corey Sandler
Welcome to. . . Internet: From Mystery to Mastery
New York: MIS Pr., 1993.
324 p., paper. ISBN 1-558-28308-0.

Braun, Eric
The Internet Directory
New York: Fawcett Columbine, 1994.
704 p., paper. ISBN 0-449-90898-4.

Dern, Daniel P.
The Internet Guide for New Users
New York: McGraw-Hill, 1994.
570 p., paper. ISBN 0-070-16511-4.

A Troubles Resource List

Engle, Mary E., and others
*Internet Connections: A Librarian's Guide to Dial-up Access
    and Use*
Chicago: Library and Information Technology Assn., 1993.
166 p., paper. ISBN 0-838-97677-8.

Estrada, Susan
Connecting to the Internet: A Buyer's Guide
Sebastopol, Calif.: O'Reilly & Associates, 1993.
170 p., paper. ISBN 1-565-92061-6.

Falk, Bennett
The Internet Roadmap
Alameda, Calif.: SYBEX, 1994.
263 p., paper. ISBN 0-782-11365-6.

Fisher, Sharon
Riding the Internet Highway
Carmel, Ind.: New Riders Publishing, 1993.
266 p., paper. ISBN 1-562-05192-X.

Frasse, Michael
The Mac Internet Tour Guide: Cruising the Internet the Easy Way
Chapel Hill, N.C.: Ventana Pr., 1993.
288 p., paper, with diskette. ISBN 1-556-04062-0.

Frasse, Michael
The PC Internet Tour Guide: Cruising the Internet the Easy Way
Chapel Hill, N.C.: Ventana Pr., 1994.
284 p., paper, with diskette. ISBN 1-556-04084-1.

Frasse, Michael
*The Windows Internet Tour Guide: Cruising the Internet
    the Easy Way*
Chapel Hill, N.C.: Ventana Pr., 1994.
350 p., paper, with diskette. ISBN 1-556-04081-7.

Gardner, James
*A DOS User's Guide to the Internet: E-mail, Netnews
    and File Transfer with UUCP*
Englewood Cliffs, N.J.: PTR Prentice Hall, 1994.
308 p., paper. ISBN 0-131-06873-3.

Gibbs, Mark, and Richard Smith
Navigating the Internet
Carmel, Ind.: Sams Publishing, 1993.
500 p., paper. ISBN 0-672-30362-0.

Gilster, Paul
The Internet Navigator
New York: Wiley, 1993.
470 p., paper. ISBN 0-471-59782-1.

Hardie, Edward T. L., and Vivian Neou (eds.)
Internet: Mailing Lists
Englewood Cliffs, N.J.: PTR Prentice Hall, 1993.
356 p., paper. ISBN 0-133-27941-3.

Kehoe, Brendan P.
Zen and the Art of the Internet: A Beginner's Guide
Englewood Cliffs, N.J.: PTR Prentice Hall, 1993.
2d ed., 112 p., paper. ISBN 0-130-10778-6.

Kochmer, Jonathan
Internet Passport: NorthWestNet's Guide to Our World Online
Bellevue, Wash.: NorthWestNet, 1993.
4th ed., 515 p., paper. ISBN 0-963-52810-6.

Krol, Ed
The Whole Internet User's Guide & Catalog
Sebastopol, Calif.: O'Reilly & Associates, 1992.
376 p., paper. ISBN 1-565-92025-2.

Lambert, Steve, and Walt Howe
*Internet Basics: Your Online Access to the Global Electronic
    Superhighway*
New York: Random House, 1993.
495 p., paper. ISBN 0-679-75023-1.

Lane, Elizabeth, and Craig Summerhill
*Internet Primer for Information Professionals: A Basic Guide
    to Internet Networking Technology*
Westport, Conn.: Mecklermedia, 1993.
175 p., paper. ISBN 0-887-36831-X.

LaQuey, Tracey
The Internet Companion: A Beginner's Guide to Global Networking
Reading, Mass.: Addison-Wesley, 1993.
196 p., paper. ISBN 0-201-62224-6.

Levine, John R., and Carol Baroudi
Internet for Dummies
San Mateo, Calif.: IDG Books, 1993.
355 p., paper. ISBN 1-568-84024-1.

A Troubles Resource List

Malamud, Carl
Exploring the Internet: A Technical Travelogue
Englewood Cliffs, N.J.: PTR Prentice Hall, 1992.
379 p., cloth. ISBN 0-132-96898-3.

Rutten, Peter, and others
*netGuide: Your Map to the Services, Information and
    Entertainment on the Electronic Highway*
New York: Random House Electronic Publishing, 1994.
356 p., paper. ISBN 0-679-75106-8.

Sachs, David, and Henry Stair
Hands-on Internet: A Beginning Guide for PC Users
Englewood Cliffs, N.J.: PTR Prentice Hall, 1994.
274 p., paper. ISBN 0-130-56392-7.

Commercial Online Services

If your connection to the electronic highway is via a gateway
and a commercial service, you're in luck. There's an abun-
dance of handbooks to guide you around dead ends and
one-way streets. You recoup your investment in these books
in the time saved not searching for digital directions. Here
are just a couple.

Bowen, Charles, and David Peyton
How to Get the Most out of CompuServe
New York: Bantam, 1993.
5th ed., 472 p., paper. ISBN 0-533-37185-1.

Lichty, Tom
The Official America Online Membership Kit & Tour Guide
Chapel Hill, N.C.: Ventana Pr., 1992.
405 p., paper, with diskette. ISBN 1-556-04012-4.

Philosophy

Internet philosophy? Deep digital thinking? Well, yes, some
are taking the Internet quite seriously and not just regarding
it as the next shopping mall in the sky. If you've been won-
dering about the implications of the dark side of the 'net,
these tomes can be great food for thought.

Benedikt, Michael (ed.)
Cyberspace: First Steps
Cambridge, Mass.: MIT Pr., 1991.
436 p., paper. ISBN 0-262-52177-6.

Forester, Tom, and Perry Morrison
Computer Ethics: Cautionary Tales and Ethical Dilemmas
  in Computing
Cambridge, Mass.: MIT Pr., 1994.
2d ed., 347 p., paper. ISBN 0-262-56073-9.

Sterling, Bruce
The Hacker Crackdown: Law and Disorder on the
  Electronic Frontier
New York: Bantam, 1992.
328 p., cloth. ISBN 0-553-08058-X.

Williams, Frederick, and John V. Pavlik (eds.)
The People's Right to Know: Media, Democracy, and
  the Information Highway
Hillsdale, N.J.: Lawrence Erlbaum, 1994.
258 p., paper. ISBN 0-805-81491-4.

Magazines

If you're a magazine junkie, you'll like these informative and high-spirited periodicals. They'll keep you posted on the latest in software, hardware, and, oh yes, fads online. You do want to be electronically chic, don't you?

Internet World
10/yr.
Mecklermedia Corp.
11 Ferry Ln. West
Westport, CT 06880
(203) 226-6967

Matrix News
monthly
Matrix Information & Directory Services, Inc.
1120 South Capitol of Texas Highway
Building 2, Suite 300
Austin, TX 78746
(512) 329-1087

Online
bimonthly
Online, Inc.
462 Danbury Rd.
Wilton, CT 06897-2126
(203) 761-1466

Online Access
10/yr.
Online Access
920 North Franklin St.
Chicago, IL 60610
(312) 573-1700

Wired
monthly
Wired USA, Ltd.
544 Second St.
San Francisco, CA 94107-1427
(415) 904-0660

Electronic Resources

NSF Internet Tour
a HyperCard stack, for Macintosh computers by the NSF
Network Service Center (NNSC)
>Available by `ftp.nnsc.nsf.net` in the `alug/EFF`
directory. It is also available as an ASCII file.

Big Dummy's Guide to the Internet
a HyperCard stack, for Macintosh computers
>Available in several locations on the Internet, includ-
ing `ftp.apple.com` in the `alug/EFF` directory. It is also
available as an ASCII file. To get a diskette, send a self-
addressed mailing label to Big Dummy, c/o Apple
Library Users Group, 4 Infinite Loop, MS304-2A,
Cupertino, CA 95014.

Big Dummy Update
monthly, by the Electronic Frontier Foundation (EFF)
>FTP to EFF at `ftp.eff.org` posted in `pub/Net_`
`info/Big_Dummy/Updates` or Gopher to
`gopher.eff.org` or by World Wide Web
`http:///www.eff.org/pub/Net_info/Big_`
`Dummy/Updates/`
>To subscribe, send a message to Big-Dummy-Update-
Request@eff.org with the message `add big-dummy-`
`update` (don't include your name!).

Digital Information Infrastructure Guide (DIIG)
updated irregularly, by the Research Program on Communications and Policy, Massachusetts Institute of Technology
(diig@farnsworth.mit.edu)

Information on the National Information Infrastructure (NII), available by Gopher at `farnsworth.mit.edu`
`port 70` or by World Wide Web at `http://farns-`
`worth.mit.edu/`.

Directory of Scholarly Electronic Conferences
updated irregularly, by the Directory Team at
kentvm.kent.edu (Diane Kovacs, Editor-in-Chief,
dkovacs@kentvm.kent.edu)

FTP to `ksuvxa.kent.edu` posted in the `library` direc-
tory and retrieve files labeled ACADLIST.README,
ACADSTAC.HQX, ACADSMAL.HQX, ACADLIST
FILE1 through FILE8, and ACADLIST CHANGES.
Alternatively, you can send a message to LISTSERV@
KENTVM or listserv@kentvm.kent.edu. Do not enter text
on subject line. Type the message `GET <filename>`
`<filetype>` such as `GET ACADSMAL HQX`.

Information Resources on the Network
updated irregularly, by Merit Network, Inc.

FTP to Merit at `nic.merit.edu` to locate the following selected files:

`fyi_01.text` FYI on F.Y.I.: Introduction to the F.Y.I.
Notes (7,722 bytes),

`fyi_03.text` FYI on Where to Start: A Bibliography of
Internetworking Information (95,238 bytes),

`fyi_04.text` FYI on Questions and Answers: Answers
to Commonly Asked "New Internet User" Questions
(71,232 bytes),

`fyi_05.text` Choosing a Name for Your Computer
(18,175 bytes),

`fyi_07.text` FYI on Questions and Answers: Answers
to Commonly Asked "Experienced Internet User"
Questions (32,829 bytes),

`fyi_09.text` Who's Who in the Internet: Biographies of
IAB, IESG Members (71,611 bytes),

`fyi_10.text` There's Gold in Them Thar Networks:
Searching for Treasure in All the Wrong Places
(71,176 bytes),

`fyi_16.text` Connecting to the Internet: What
Connecting Institutions Should Anticipate
(53,449 bytes),

`fyi_18.text` Internet Users' Glossary (104,624 bytes),

`fyi_19.text` Introducing the Internet—A Short Bibliography of Introductory Internetworking Reading for the Network Novice (7,116 bytes),

`fyi_20.text` What Is the Internet? (27,811 bytes), and

`fyi_21.text` FYI on Questions and Qnswers: Answers to Commonly Asked "Primary and Secondary School Internet User" Questions (113,646 bytes).

The Internet Hunt
monthly, by Rick Gates (rgates@ccit.arizona.edu)
Gopher to `gopher.cic.net` and choose `The Internet Hunt` from the menu.

GLOSSARY

A Beginning
Glossary of Internet
and Related Terms

This glossary is decidedly not definitive or comprehensive. It is designed to help novices grasp a few of the tens of thousands of terms floating around on networks. If you don't understand a term or phrase as you roam electronically, ask another networker; most will be happy to explain or tell a story, or point you in the right direction for a definition.

There are a number of excellent dictionaries of computer, telecommunications, networking, and electronics terminology. Several are listed in our Resource List, including two recent volumes worth a second mention here for their reference and entertainment values. More than mere mortal dictionaries are Eric Raymond's *The New Hacker's Dictionary* (Cambridge, Mass.: MIT Pr., 1993) and Robin Williams and Steve Cummings's *Jargon: An Informal Dictionary of Computer Terms* (Berkeley, Calif.: Peachpit Pr., 1993).

address On the Internet both you and your computer are uniquely identified by a set of characters so that information can find its way across networks. An Internet address is a 32-bit number defined by the Internet Protocol for a computer, represented in decimals. Those decimals usually appear in the form 012.345.67.89, with each digit representing 8 bits of the address. Users have a more difficult time with strings of numbers, so addresses appear in more human terms, such as well.sf.ca.us.

anonymous FTP Anonymous File Transfer Protocol, a means to access another computer and its files via the Internet. A local program acts as an FTP client to reach an FTP server on another machine. Once the connection is made, a login is required with a password. Since passwords are not abundantly available for remote computers, a special login called "anonymous" allows anyone to reach certain FTP-accessible files. Anonymous logins usually require a password, usually corresponding to a user's e-mail address.

archie An Internet tool used to discover anonymous FTP sites It was originally invented at McGill University and exists as a database posted on archie servers throughout the world.

ASCII An acronym meaning the American Standard Code for Information Interchange. Standard ASCII includes all upper- and lower-case roman characters, all numbers, punctuation marks, and some special codes used in programming and telecommunications. Extended ASCII includes diacritical marks, certain line segments, and mathematical symbols. When you save a file in ASCII in your word processor, you make it possible for other computers and programs to read your file.

asynchronous transmission Eavesdrop on a conversation. Humans rarely talk to each other simultaneously; we usually wait for one person to speak, and then reply. This sort of communication is asynchronous. Computers talk to each other the same way, sending files to each other at different times and intervals. We know in a conversation when a sentence or phrase begins or ends by verbal and nonverbal signals. Computers know when to send and when not to send, with special signals indicating when a message starts and when it stops. Some computers speak synchronously just as some humans do, as in any movie version of *The Front Page.* It's unlikely you'll encounter synchronous computers in most normal travel on networks.

baud rate The speed at which messages are sent between computers by modems. This speed is usually measured in the number of bits per second. A bit is the smallest unit of information handled by a computer, and 8 bits make a byte. Modems can ship messages around at 1200, 2400, or 9600 baud, and faster modems are becoming increasingly common. Computer purists will be happy to point out that baud and bps are not the same, so don't use these terms interchangeably. You might be flamed.

bit The short form of binary digit, it is the tiniest unit of information that a computer can understand, or a 0 or 1.

BITNET Because It's There Network, also Because It's Time Network. The network of IBM mainframes that includes BITNET in the U.S. and Mexico, EARN in Europe, and NETNORTH in Canada. BITNET nodes are distinctive by their length of 8 characters or less, such as UICVM, compared to a long-winded Internet version, such as uicvm.uic.edu.

bps An acronym meaning bits per second, a reference to speed at which computers or their devices talk to each other. Printers, storage devices, and other peripherals transfer data at speeds measured in bps, so this term applies to any transfer of information from one locale to another.

A Beginning Glossary of Internet and Related Terms

BTW Shorthand in electronic correspondence meaning "By the Way," as in "BTW, have you seen the latest flame on . . . ?"

byte Eight bits collected as a unit. One byte might present a single alphanumeric character on your computer monitor. A collection of 4,000 bytes might equal a single page of double-spaced text in your word processor.

carriage return-line feed ASCII characters used to indicate the end of line or record. Also called newline.

case-sensitive. The nature of certain applications and operating systems to react differently to characters in upper- or lower-case. Unix is case-sensitive, so Ed.txt, ed.txt and Ed.Txt may produce different (and unexpected) responses.

character set Numbers, letters, punctuation, and special characters form character sets. ASCII is one kind of common character set used by computers.

client Used to describe a computer that is seeking data from another computer (the server). The client machine often runs some special software which speaks the server's jargon. Clients often depend on servers for files which are too large or complex for their own local computing resources. Client programs also make using a server easier by employing the common features of their operating environment (e.g., windows, scroll bars).

client/server model A way in which software is configured on a network, allowing certain computers, or clients, to request information and work from certain other computers, or servers. Servers are prepared to handle these requests while performing other tasks. For example, when you use WHOIS, an Internet resource, you start a client program locally by the command `WHOIS Vale`. The client software makes a request to the WHOIS server for information, once you've cleared the server's requirements for WHOIS. It answers the client's request, and sends the information to you.

CMS Conversational Monitor System. A mainframe system that runs under the VM—Virtual Machine—Operating System to provide basic user services such as file management, file editing, and electronic mail.

crash The complete and sudden failure of a computer's operating system. Also known as a system crash.

daemon An application operating in the background. In the client/server model, servers often have programs or daemons that run in the background in response to requests from local or remote clients for work or information.

databits Data shipped over a modem are composed of seven or eight bits per character. The default setting is eight bits.

DECnet The proprietary networking protocol invented by the Digital Equipment Corporation for its computers; not compatible with the Internet.

DNS Domain Name System, a way to explain the location of computers in a non-numerical way. The order of information in a name provides clues on the location of users and their computers. The most specific information is to the far left, the most general to the right. In the address `uicvm.uic.edu`, `uicvm` refers to a specific computer at the University of Illinois at Chicago (`uic`), an educational institution (`edu`).

domain names A set of characters found at the far right of an Internet address providing, in the United States, general information about an organization. `.edu` refers to educational institutions, as in `mit.edu`; `.gov` belongs to federal agencies, such as `lanl.gov` for the Los Alamos National Laboratory in New Mexico; `.mil` describes military groups; `.net` labels network administration such as `nwnet.net` or NorthWestNet in Redmond, Washington; `.org` for not-for-profit organizations such as `ala.org`, indicating the American Library Association; and `.com` correlating to for-profit organizations such as `apple.com` or Apple Computer. These codes can identify a specific country. For example, `.nl` equals the Netherlands, `.uk` the United Kingdom, `.au` for Australia, `.ch` for Switzerland and `.us` for the United States.

duplex Not a reference to a housing complex, but instead a message to the computer that indicates how you would like to see (or not see) characters echoed on your monitor.

EARN European Academic Research Network, the equivalent of BITNET in Europe.

EBCDIC The IBM-proprietary Extended Binary Coded Decimal Interchange Code an eight-bit code, by which IBM mainframes understand characters. To move files from a mainframe to a personal computer, a file conversion utility will translate from EBCDIC to ASCII.

electronic mail or e-mail Correspondence sent by individuals to colleagues via computer networks. This mail may consist of text, graphics, or audio files—or combinations of all three types of files. In addition, programs can also be shipped easily over networks to other users. Electronic mail offers several advantages, including speed of transmission, security, and low cost, in comparison with other forms of communication.

emoticons Also known as smileys. A typographic shorthand, created to express emotion, especially humor, anger, disgust, or boredom. The basic character (to be viewed sideways) is known as a smiley or :-) and variations can use several combinations of keyboard characters.

emulation The imitation by one computing device or program of another device or program, in order to permit transparent access to networked resources. One of the most common telecommunications emulations is VT100, coined in respect to a popular DEC terminal. A client displays information from a server as if it was a VT100 terminal, and the server treats the input—that is, keyboard input—from the client as if the computer was a VT100 terminal.

encryption A technique to translate information into a form that is unintelligible by any device without the proper decoding software and hardware.

escape sequence A command issued to regain attention of keyboard and screen that otherwise are dedicated to some started process.

Ethernet A standard means to permit computers to form networks. The setup consists of an Ethernet card in each computer on the network, special cable between computers, and software to provide a common interface for all devices.

exporting The act of moving information from one type of program to another similar program, such as migrating text from one word processor to another.

FAQ Frequently Asked Questions. A text file describing an Internet resource in a series of questions with answers.

file Information pulled together as a coherent unit. A file may contain text, graphics, and other kinds of information, linked to create a logical and intelligible statement.

file conversion The transfer of the contents of one file into another file, changing file formats but not altering the underlying information.

file extension A code at the end of a file name, providing a clue to the kind of information contained in a file. For instance, `.txt` identifies text, `.ps` a PostScript file, and `.tif` represents a graphics format.

finger A means to check which users have valid accounts on a specific computer system, and which are currently logged on. The form of the request is `finger <user ID>@<node>`. Also, *finger* can be used to secure a list of all who are logged onto a system at any given moment; the command is `finger @<node>`. *finger* can also provide brief descriptions of resources. Not all computers appreciate fingers, nor do their users!

flame A verb, meaning to send an emotionally charged network message, usually characterized by anger, ridicule, or sarcasm. A person who flames a great deal is known as a flamer, not the most admired sort. Flamers often like to start flame wars by writing a provocative message or sending "flame bait" to a public group. Flame wars are like those bar fights in old westerns, where one cowboy insults another and soon the entire room is trashed. An entire message does not necessarily have to be flammable. A small portion of a text could be devoted to a flame; the author will usually indicate this transfer from normal communication to flame, by indicating "`flame on`" and "`flame off`." Of course, there are ways to protect yourself from flames, by announcing that you are donning, in the virtual sense, an asbestos coat or other asbestos-lined material.

FTP File Transfer Protocol. A technique or protocol for getting network-accessible files. The protocol depends upon the user having an FTP client and the target system running the FTP server software. See also **anonymous FTP**.

full duplex In telecommunications, the transmission of information by two computers simultaneously. Both computers actually send and receive data at the same time over their physical connection.

GIF or giff Graphics Interchange Format. Developed by CompuServe, a way to compress, store, and send graphics files over networks. A utility translates and decompresses GIF files, making them usable on a specific computer.

gigabyte G or GB or Gb, the equivalent of 1,024 megabytes, or more than one billion bytes.

Gopher Also called Internet Gopher. An Internet resource retrieval tool developed at the University of Minnesota (whose mascot is the Gopher). Gopher is characterized by its connectionless protocol, i.e., each request for data between a Gopher client and server is its own complete exchange. The connection to the remote system's Gopher server is not left open. Gopher clients and servers come in different flavors of operating systems, e.g., Mac, Unix.

GUI Graphical User Interface, where icons, menus, and symbols are used to represent files, commands, and other information, such as is found on the Macintosh.

hacker A person devoted to the use of computers, above many other considerations.

half duplex In telecommunications, the state when information is exchanged between computers with each device taking a turn in sending data over a connection.

handshaking The means by which two computers agree to talk to each other.

header In electronic mail, the text found before the actual contents of a message. It describes the sender and the sender's computers, the path a message followed to a specific location, the subject of the contents, and a date stamp.

hypertext A method for embedding special links in documents. The links connect the intellectual contents of a document to other documents and files in real time. World Wide Web is considered one of the most successful implementations of the concept of hypertext.

import To bring information into a single file from another file or set of files. In the electronic file of this book, text and illustrations were imported to create a coherent whole.

A Beginning Glossary of Internet and Related Terms

infect To take a malicious computer program known as a virus, bug, or Trojan horse and disguise it on a system, in order to transport it to other systems or cause havoc on local operating systems and applications.

Internet No, it's not a digital superhighway or a country road. It's a collection of millions of computers, tens of thousands of networks, some 20 million users, cables, phone lines, satellite transmissions, standards, and protocols. A byzantine collection of hardware, software, and people, representing a paean to the very human need to communicate as quickly and as effortlessly as possible.

Internet address Your specific combination of characters that locates you in cyberspace. The first part of the address, or user ID, locates you; e.g., `vvvale` in `vvvale@well.sf.ca.us`. The remaining portion, or node, tells other computers and correspondents which computer contains your electronic mailbox.

IP Internet Protocol, the network layer in the TCP/IP Protocol.

ISDN Integrated Services Digital Network, a communications system replacing current telephone communications with digital connections.

JPEG Joint Photographic Experts Group, a compression format for graphics.

Kermit A telecommunications protocol used to emulate a terminal and to send files from one computer to another, but especially mainframe files to personal computers. Named, with permission, after the frog.

kilobyte K or KB, equivalent to 1,024 bytes.

lha Also known as lharc, a compression utility for DOS files.

LISTSERV An IBM mainframe computer program written by Eric Thomas that supports the distribution of files and mail messages to groups or subscribers. LISTSERV is also used generically to describe other software programs that accomplish the same set of tasks: subscription, distribution, statistics.

local area network LAN, a group of computers linked together by cable rather than telecommunications software and phone or satellite connections.

login Also known as log on. The set of commands to gain access to another computer, network, or online service, which includes some sort of personal identification and password.

ls A Unix command to list files in a specific directory.

lurk A verb, applied to those who read but do not reply nor post new messages on a public forum. To lurk or to describe yourself as a lurker is not bad; everyone is a lurker to some extent on the Internet. Networks don't have the capacity for everyone to express themselves on everything, and we don't have the capacity to digest it all in any case.

megabyte MB, equivalent to one million bytes.

megahertz MHz, or a million cycles per second, often seen in reference to the clock speed of computers where a device is noted to operate at, say, 60 MHz.

MIPS Million Instructions per Second, a measure of the speed of a computer in terms of its processing capabilities.

modem From <u>mo</u>dulator-<u>de</u>modulator. An external or internal device attached to your computer that translates digital information into analog form and back again, so computers can communicate over phone lines. Modems require some sort of telecommunications software to work properly. This software acts as an interface between your computer and your modem, and other computers and their communications software.

Mosaic A client of the hypertext system known as World Wide Web.

MVS Multiple Virtual Storage, the operating system of IBM mainframes beginning with OS/360.

netnews An informal description of newsgroups distributed to the Internet. It is also the name of a specific news reader for VM systems.

network The means for one computer or device to work and communicate with another. Connections may involve a combination of software and hardware to allow all computing devices to operate harmoniously.

newsgroups Bulletin boards on the Internet created on specialized topics. Postings are read by subscribers on a global basis, in some cases. Some newsgroups are moderated.

node A computer attached to and offering services on the Internet. Your node is part of your Internet address, as a reference to the information after the @ sign. For example, in the address `u25112@uicvm.uic.edu`, `uicvm` refers to a computer at the the educational institution known as UIC, or the University of Illinois at Chicago.

noise In telecommunications, interference that complicates instructions between computers. It may be caused by human accidents, electronic devices, or cosmic events such as solar flares.

NSFnet The National Science Foundation network, backbone of the Internet and originally designed to make supercomputer centers accessible to researchers. The network consists of several layers, connecting local and regional networks to a larger national network, and in turn providing a means to connect with networks in other parts of the world.

null modem Literally, without modem. Can be just a special cable, or simply cables and an adapter. A technique to connect two computers via the modem port of each device to quickly exchange information.

A Beginning Glossary of Internet and Related Terms

offline Not connected to a network.

offline device Any peripheral not part of the network at any given moment.

online Connected to one or more computers via a combination of hardware such as a modem and software.

online device Any computing instrument available on a network.

operating system The basic instructions that make a computer functional for humans and other computers.

output device A printer or other tool such as a monitor that provides information from computers for humans.

packet The basic unit of information sent across a network.

parallel port The physical connection that allows your computer to have connected to it a parallel protocol device, such as a printer. See also **serial port**.

parity Error checking on the part of your software and computer when you communicate with other computers. If you're set for 8 databits, you won't need parity.

PKZIP A compression program on DOS computers. Also allows for several files to be collected together into one. There is also a GNU version. See also **zip**.

port A connection between a computer and a transmission line, such as a modem.

PostScript A language that describes pages, created by Adobe Systems.

PPP Point-to-Point Protocol, a means to send packets over point-to-point connections between computers.

program Instructions that operate a computer or peripheral.

protocol Standards that define rules that govern how computers will communicate with each other. TCP/IP and Kermit are examples of protocols.

RFC Request for Comments, or working drafts of the Internet research and development community.

router A computing vehicle to transfer files and other information between networks.

sea Self-Extracting Archive, a file extension for a compressed file that will decompress itself without the original compression utility.

serial port The connection, or port, that allows your modem to connect to your computer. It is called "serial" because data move through this port bit by single bit. On DOS and other computers, serial ports are known as COM1, COM2, COM3, and COM4. On the Macintosh and some other computers, this port may be represented by an icon.

servers Computers on networks, providing access to programs and files for local and remote users.

service providers Outlets to the Internet are known as service providers. In the United States, there are national providers such as CLASS (Cooperative Library Agency for Systems and Services) in San Jose, California; UUNET in Falls Church, Virginia; or the WELL (Whole Earth 'Lectronic Link) in Sausalito, California. Regional providers concentrate on one part of the country, such as NorthWestNet for the northwestern region of the U.S., or a single state, such as netILLINOIS or MSEN for Michigan. The kind of Internet service you receive varies from provider to provider, depending on location, services needed, and costs.

SLIP Serial Line Internet Protocol, a means to operate IP over telephone lines or cables, expanding the connections of computers to networks.

smileys See **emoticons**.

SMTP Simple Mail Transfer Protocol, a vehicle for mail to be sent around the Internet, between servers.

stop bits A signal sent by one computer to another to indicate that a byte has been sent. Stop bits are usually set to 1.

TCP/IP Transmission Control Protocol/Internet Protocol, a descriptor for a whole suite of communications protocols linking computers together on the Internet.

telnet Terminal emulation over the Internet allowing remote access to computing resources.

terminal emulation Before computers became very smart, they had to talk to big mainframe computers in a certain way, as if they were just a dumb terminal hooked up to the Big Iron. Even though desktop computers have become quite intelligent in their own ways, mainframes still expect them to act dumb in certain predictable ways, before any communication occurs. Probably the most common and safest emulation is VT100, a terminal once constructed by DEC (Digital Equipment Corporation). Variations on this include VT52, VT102, and TTY (or TeleTYpewriter).

tiff Tagged Image File Format, a file format for scanned images.

Trojan horse A computer program that acts as a harmless application, but eventually causes damage to files and operating systems.

tty TeleTYpewriter, a device containing both printer and keyboard in one unit. Often seen as an emulation choice in some telecommunications software.

txt A file extension referring to a file containing only text.

Unix An operating system that operates on a number of computing platforms, consisting of the kernel, the shell or interface, and the file system.

unzip To uncompress zip files compressed with the utility PKZip.

Usenet A formal description for sets of newsgroups distributed to computers and their users over the Internet.

utility A small program that provides an improvement in certain computing routines.

UUCP Unix-to-Unix Copying Program, a way in Unix for one computer to send information to another Unix-based computer over telephone line connections. It now describes a network which distributes data by the UUCP protocol.

vaccine A computer application created to combat computer viruses and most notably warn users of a potential problem with a file or application.

virus A computer program hidden in other computer programs with the sole intent of causing damage to files and operating systems.

WAIS Wide Area Information Servers. An Internet protocol that allows remote clients to search for information on servers running the protocol. WAIS is characterized by its ability to index full text, to handle natural language queries, and to rank retrieved items for relevance based on the words in the query.

WAN Wide Area Network, computers connected over a large geographic area.

WHOIS A means to locate an individual in the Network Information Center (NIC), e.g., the command WHOIS <Last-Name>. Names are stored in the file in order of last name first, then first name. You can search for a portion of a name by using a period to abbreviate a search, as in WHOIS vala. for WHOIS valauskas.

XModem A protocol for transferring data from one personal computer to another.

Xon/Xoff A way of one computer telling another computer to stop sending information until processing of incoming data is completed.

X.25 A specification of how information moves over public networks.

YModem A means for sending data between computers over telephone lines with a modem.

ZIP An identification of a compressed file created by PKZip.

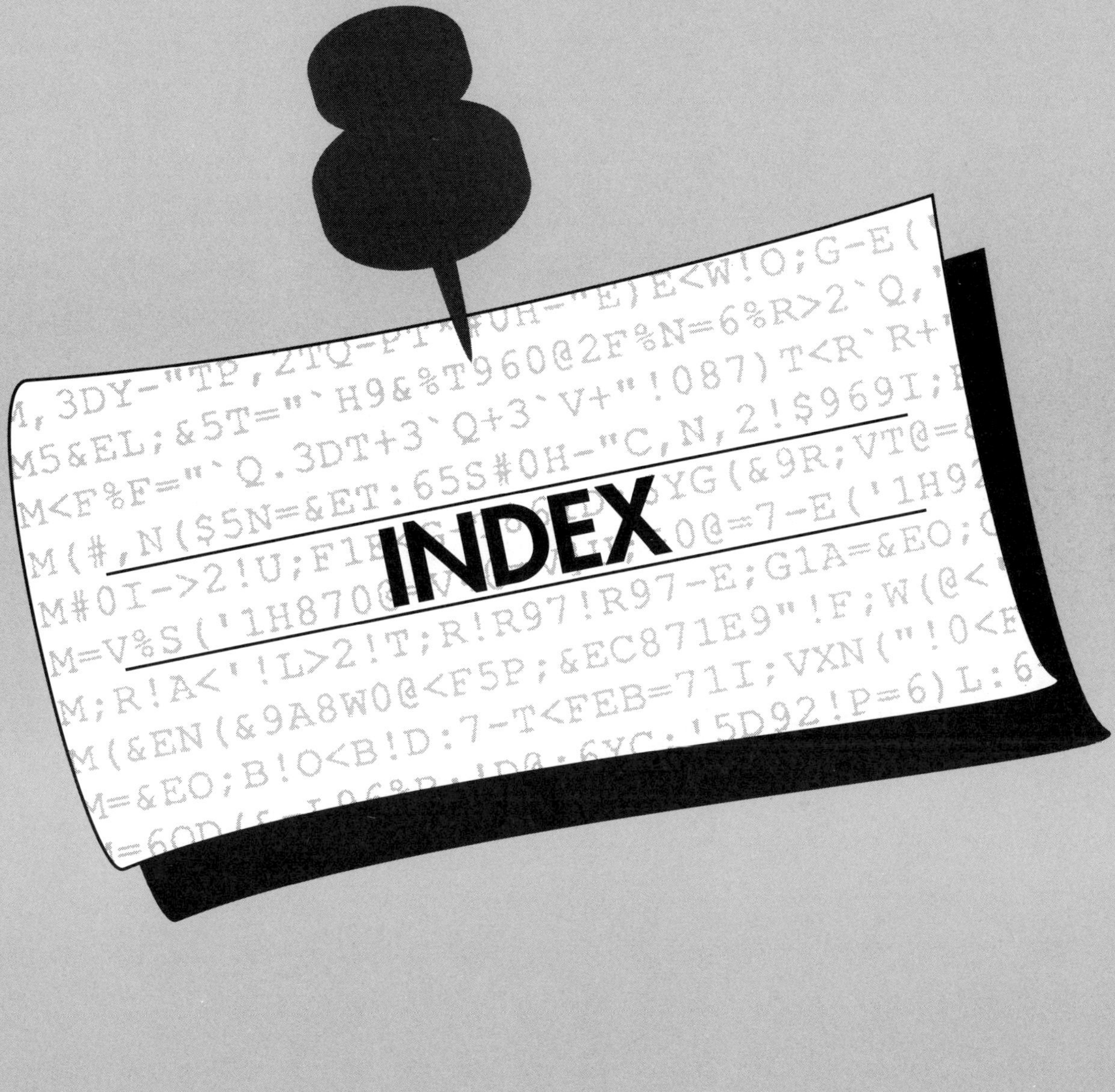
INDEX

Index

The authors are experienced information managers and educators who have taught hundreds of Internet users at every level.

Nancy R. John is assistant university librarian at the University of Illinois at Chicago. As manager of library systems, she has been an active Internet user and troubleshooter. A member of the American Library Association, she is active in the U.S. Gopher community. Her current research is a study of veronica's words.

Edward J. Valauskas, consultant and author on information technology, is principal in Internet Mechanics, a consulting firm. An Internet consultant and instructor at the American Library Association headquarters in Chicago, he writes columns for *Online, Database, Library Journal,* and the *Newsletter* of the Apple Library Users Group. He is the founder and co-editor of *Macintoshed Libraries,* a series of annual publications about the Macintosh computer in libraries.

The authors welcome your comments on *The Internet Troubleshooter* and suggestions for future editions.

nancy.john@uic.edu
edward.valauskas@ala.org